Raglan Castle

John R. Kenyon BA, MCLIP, FSA, FRHistS

A History of Raglan Castle

Introduction

Raglan was one of the last medieval castles to be built in England and Wales, though palace-fortress might be a better description. With its crisp silhouette crowning the ridge amid a glorious pastoral landscape, it remains one of the finest late medieval buildings set within the remains of one of the most elaborate Renaissance gardens in the British Isles. Yet we can, too, look at Raglan with a feeling of some regret. Compare Thomas Churchyard's poetic description of the castle in its great Elizabethan days with Sir Richard Colt Hoare's comment in his journal for 7 June 1802, which emphasizes the tragedy that befell the site in the intervening period. Although it is no longer neglected, had it not been for the Civil War in the 1640s Raglan's magnificence would undoubtedly have been that much greater.

Not farre from thence, a famous Castle fine,
That Ragland hight, stands moted almost round:
Made of Freestone, upright as straight as line,
Whose workmanship, in beautie doth abound.
The curious knots, wrought all with edged toole,
The stately Tower, that lookes ore Pond and Poole:
The Fountaine trim, that runs both day and night,
Doth yeeld in showe, a rare and noble sight.

Thomas Churchyard, *The Worthines of Wales* (1587)

I cannot but regret whenever I view this grand relict of baronial magnificence that it has been so long neglected and uninhabited.

Sir Richard Colt Hoare, *Journeys … through England and Wales, 1793–1810*

Origins: The Bloets

Raglan lies in the old Welsh border district of Gwent. Following the Norman Conquest of England, when the invaders were beginning to advance into Wales, the area was in the hands of William fitz Osbern, earl of Hereford (d. 1071), who established a number of castles along the southern March, including those at Chepstow and Monmouth. We cannot be sure whether an earth-and-timber castle was established at Raglan at this time, but it is worth noting that the present castle dominates most of the immediate area and stands guard close to where the old Chepstow to Abergavenny road crosses the Gloucester to Monmouth road, leading eventually to Usk and Caerleon. Not only did this prominent site afford a strategic location but it also provided the occupants with fine views of the surrounding countryside and the hills beyond.

It is just possible that the detached main tower or keep at Raglan — the 'Yellow Tower of Gwent' — may be on the site of a large flat-topped mound or motte, with the curving line of the surrounding buildings occupying the site of the bailey or courtyard. Indeed, in 1959, part of a ditch — assumed to be that of the bailey — was revealed close to the Closet Tower.

By 1172, the lord of Chepstow, Earl Richard de Clare (d. 1176) — better known as 'Strongbow' — had granted Raglan to Walter Bloet (or Bluet), probably in recognition of his services in Ireland. At this time Raglan lay in the lordship of Usk and was held by military tenure, Bloet being required to provide his overlord with the service of one knight. The male line of the Bloet family continued to hold Raglan until the late fourteenth century when, on the death of Sir John Bloet, it passed to his only daughter, Elizabeth. Documents survive which provide us with some evidence for the manor house, the home of the Bloets, before the fifteenth-century castle was built.

Opposite: Raglan Castle — 'this grand relict of baronial magnificence' — from the north-west. Despite centuries of depredation, Raglan remains one of the finest late medieval buildings in the British Isles: testament to the power, wealth and status of the Herbert family and their successors, the Somersets, earls of Worcester.

Penrhos Farm motte-and-bailey castle, about 3 miles (5km) north of Raglan. A similar earthwork fortification may have preceded the later stone-built stronghold at Raglan.

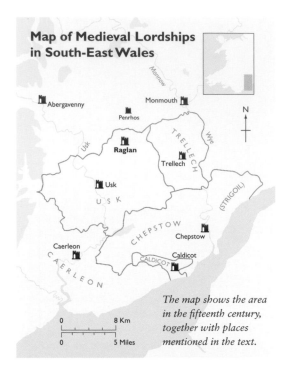

Map of Medieval Lordships in South-East Wales

The map shows the area in the fifteenth century, together with places mentioned in the text.

A section from an account roll of 1375/76 recording expenditure on repairs to the manorial buildings at Raglan (Public Record Office, SC 6/925/4).

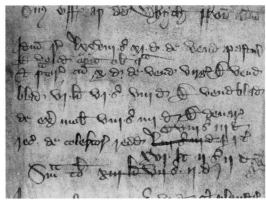

One of the late thirteenth-century tiles found during restoration work in the 1940s, which suggest the presence of a chapel at the Bloet period manor.

A record of 1354 mentions that it was the custom, when the lord of Raglan was in residence, for the reeve (an estate official) to eat his meals in the lord's hall with the other officers of the household. Further details appear in an account roll of 1375/76, which lists various minor repairs undertaken following storm damage, including work on a chamber and the hall roof. The same account records the cost (9*d.*) for a hook and hinge for the door of the latrine attached to the 'Lord's Chamber'. There is also evidence for a chapel at the manor house, for, during clearance of the castle in the 1940s, thirteenth-century paving tiles were found in the area of the known fifteenth-century chapel. In all, we have

here a manorial complex — hall, chapel, private accommodation and service buildings — grouped around at least one courtyard, the layout of which almost certainly dictated the plan of the fifteenth-century castle.

Associated with the Bloet manor in the fourteenth century was a park, possibly the Home Park of later records. Its existence is known from the 1375/76 document, where payment is made to a man for clearing part of the park of trees and pasture so that it could be ploughed and sowed for corn. The necessity to hedge the new field suggests that the corn needed to be protected from animals, possibly deer or cattle kept in the park. The manorial pond is also mentioned, as well as a mill. The management of the surrounding landscape in this way served both economic and aesthetic purposes; gardens enhanced the immediate environs, as well as the status of the owners, and parkland provided grazing for deer, a source of food for the table as well as sport.

Raglan came into the possession of Sir James Berkeley upon his marriage to Elizabeth Bloet, and he was confirmed in his holding as lord of Raglan in 1399. In 1406, just after Sir James's death, Elizabeth, 'the lady of Raggeland', of Welsh descent herself, took as her second husband William ap Thomas (d.1445), and presumably lived in the Bloet manor house until her death in 1420. It was this William ap Thomas who began to build the castle as we see it today.

Sir William ap Thomas: The Castle Begun

William was the fifth son of a minor Welsh gentry family but soon demonstrated his ambition to establish himself as a person of consequence in south Wales. He was destined to become a supreme example of how leaders of regional Welsh society came to occupy key positions in the governance of mid-fifteenth-century Wales. As early as 1421 William held the important position of steward of the lordship of Abergavenny, and in 1426 he was knighted by Henry VI (1422–61; 1470–71), becoming known to his compatriots as *'y marchog glas o Went'* ('the blue knight of Gwent').

During 1442–43 he became the chief steward of the duke of York's estates in Wales. Other positions

The arms of Sir William ap Thomas (above), halved with those of his second wife, Gwladus, daughter of the celebrated Dafydd Gam, who perished at the battle of Agincourt in 1415 (Cardiff Central Library, Ms. 5.7). Sir William also fought at Agincourt — shown below in a fifteenth-century French manuscript illustration — and no doubt profited from the war with France (V&A Picture Library).

held by Sir William included that of the sheriff of Cardiganshire and Carmarthenshire, to which he was appointed in 1435, and his appointment as sheriff of Glamorgan followed in 1440. Although he became one of the followers of Richard, duke of York (d. 1460), who was lord of Usk, and a member of the duke's military council, Sir William's sphere of influence was largely confined to south Wales. Nevertheless, his association with the House of York laid the foundations on which his son, William Herbert (d. 1469), was to build a position of considerable power.

Following the death of his wife, Elizabeth, William ap Thomas continued to hold Raglan as a tenant of his own stepson, James, Lord Berkeley, and in 1425 the latter agreed that his stepfather could retain Raglan for the duration of his life. William married for a second time, and chose another heiress, Gwladus (d. 1454), the daughter of Dafydd Gam (the famous opponent of Owain Glyn Dŵr) and the widow of

Sir Roger Vaughan of Bredwardine in Herefordshire. Both of these men had been part of the Welsh contingent that fought with King Henry V (1413–22) in France and were killed at the battle of Agincourt in 1415, where William ap Thomas had also fought and no doubt gained profits that enhanced his standing.

By 1432 Sir William was in a position to purchase the manor of Raglan from the Berkeleys for 1,000 marks (almost £667, the modern equivalent being about £300,000), and it was probably from this time that he began to build the castle as we know it today. Perhaps with the exception of the hall range, which Sir William may have modified but was later largely rebuilt, the building programme eventually swept away the original structures of the Bloet's manor house. The principal buildings surviving from the time of Sir William are the South Gate — which may have been the main approach to the castle at this time — and probably the Great Tower, both equipped with primitive gunloops.

The Great Tower is an impressive self-contained fortress-cum-residence, lying outside the circuit of the curtain walls and surrounded by a moat. It dominates the rest of the castle physically and symbolically; it is the inner sanctum to which the lord of Raglan could withdraw or retreat. But without written records it is difficult to be certain who built it. Two sources appear to favour Sir William ap Thomas: first, a poem in praise of William by the fifteenth-century poet, Guto'r Glyn, mentions the tower at Raglan which 'stands above all other buildings'. Although one has to be wary of bardic panegyrics, this is likely to be the Great Tower for, as we have seen, there is no certain evidence for an earlier stone keep (p. 3). Secondly, a late seventeenth-century Herbert family chronicle known as the *Herbertorum Prosapia*, written by Sir Thomas Herbert of Tintern, makes reference to Raglan where Sir William:

… had erected a Tower of great Breadth and height proportionable of severall aequilateral sides and angles, about which was an artificiall Graft or Trench filled with water. This was named Sir Willm Thomas his Tower.

Such family tradition has to be considered seriously.

Nevertheless, similarities have been observed in the decorative masonry — for example, in the fireplaces and windows — in the two phases represented by the work of William ap Thomas and

his son, William Herbert. Herbert was altogether wealthier and politically more powerful than his father, and able not only to cement his position as the most important Welshman in south Wales, but also to uphold the position of the new Yorkist king, Edward IV (1461–70, 1471–83). His standing, combined with the architectural evidence, has led some authorities to suggest that Herbert rather than his father was responsible for the Great Tower. Indeed, a document of 1599, probably by a herald of the College of Arms, states that Herbert 'bulded the Castell of Raglan', but this of course need not

preclude Sir William ap Thomas's involvement in the construction of the Great Tower.

Sir William ap Thomas died in London in 1445 and was succeeded by his eldest son, William, who took the surname Herbert. Sir William's body was brought back to Wales to be buried in the Benedictine priory church at Abergavenny. His wife, Gwladus, 'y seren o Efenni' ('the star of Abergavenny'), as she was hailed by the poet Lewys Glyn Cothi, died in 1454 and was laid to rest beside him. The poet tells us — perhaps with some pardonable poetic exaggeration — that no less than 3,000 mourners attended her funeral.

The Great Tower (in the foreground), the South Gate (left) and parts of the hall range (centre) date from the time of Sir William ap Thomas and probably lie close to or incorporate the remains of the Bloet manor. It has been suggested that the island on which the Great Tower is built may be the remains of a motte and that the walls of the Fountain and Pitched Stone Courts follow the line of the former castle bailey (Crown copyright: RCAHMW).

Sir William Herbert, Earl of Pembroke: A Palatial Residence

William Herbert was destined to play a major role in the affairs of state during the opening years of the reign of Edward IV, but perhaps because of his short life, he has tended to be overshadowed in historical terms by the Lancastrian, Jasper Tudor, earl of Pembroke (1452–61; 1485–95) and half-brother to Henry VI.

Herbert came to hold a position of great power in Wales as the premier supporter of the House of York; indeed, the poet Lewys Glyn Cothi hailed him as 'King Edward's master-lock' in that land (*'unclo'r Cing Edwart yw'r Herbart hwn'*). He was arguably one of the most important Welshmen — if not the most important — of his generation, a man who might be seen as giving Wales an important role in the turbulent politics of the mid-fifteenth century. Indeed, he was viewed by the poets as the leading candidate to fulfil the role of 'national deliverer', who would free Wales from the control of the English yoke. We see him consolidating the family's rise to great power and wealth by taking the name Herbert, claiming a (fictitious) descent from one Herbert ap Godwin, an illegitimate son of King Henry I (1100–35), a descent upheld by an inquisition of about 1461. At the request of the king this enquiry was attended by 'four of the choicest learned men in pedigrees within the province of Southwals' and the ensuing report was written in no less than three languages: Welsh, Latin and French.

William Herbert served in France, as his father had done, and was captured in 1450 at the battle of Formigny. Presumably his release was dependent on the payment of a ransom. Two years later, he was knighted, and seems to have spent the 1450s consolidating his estates and building up his trade connections with France and the Low Countries, his ships bringing wine from Gascony to the port of Bristol. From about 1460, Sir William became a leading figure in national affairs. In that year he was confirmed as sheriff of Glamorgan and constable of Usk Castle as a reward for not supporting the Yorkist cause at the rout of Ludford Bridge in October 1459.

In 1461, Herbert attached himself to Edward, earl of March, son of Richard, duke of York (d. 1460). During these years of strife known as the Wars of the Roses (1455–87), Herbert was the most important Welshman to throw in his lot with Edward in his bid to seize the throne. He played a leading role in the defeat of the Lancastrian forces led by Jasper Tudor at Mortimer's Cross in Herefordshire (February 1461), a battle which proved to be a decisive Yorkist victory. Within a month Edward had ascended the throne as King Edward IV, and he made the trusted Sir William chief justice and chamberlain of south Wales as a reward for his help. Later in the same year the young king created him Baron Herbert of Raglan. For much of the 1460s Herbert was concerned with the Lancastrian threat in Wales, and probably spent little time at the court in London, for it was not until 1466 that his name appears as a witness to a royal charter. Indeed, his presence at Raglan in the late 1450s and 60s is seemingly attested by accounts recording the delivery of large quantities of salt, spices, geese, hens, piglets, calves and other foodstuffs for the 'lord's kitchen and his household'.

Lord Herbert's sphere of influence eventually extended to north Wales, and he was responsible for military operations against the Lancastrians in Wales as a whole. In 1462 he was created a Knight of the Garter, and in 1467 chief justice of north Wales. Indeed, in 1462 the young Henry Tudor, the future King Henry VII (1485–1509), was placed in the custody of Sir William and his wife to be brought up at Raglan Castle. Herbert was now in a position, more than at any other time, to create the palace-fortress of Raglan, a symbol fitting for a man of his status. The castle no

Trading activities, particularly the importation of Gascon wines into the port of Bristol, added significantly to Sir William Herbert's wealth in the 1450s. This late fifteenth-century manuscript illustration shows a cargo ship unloading at a port (Bodleian Library, University of Oxford, Ms. Douce 208, f. 120v).

The arms of Sir William Herbert halved with those of his wife, Anne Devereux, from the family chronicle, the Herbertorum Prosapia *(Cardiff Central Library, Ms. 5.7).*

Opposite: Sir William Herbert (d. 1469) came to hold a position of great power in Wales. As the premier supporter of the House of York he was handsomely rewarded, the final accolade being his elevation to the peerage as earl of Pembroke in 1468. In this manuscript illustration from John Lydgate's Troy Book, *Sir William and his wife, Anne Devereux, are shown kneeling before their king and benefactor, Edward IV (1461–70, 1471–83) (British Library, Royal Ms. 18 DII, f. 6).*

The Builders and Owners of Raglan Castle

(1) Elizabeth Berkeley =	William ap Thomas =	(2) Gwladus
[Bloet heiress]	(d. 1445)	[Daughter of Dafydd Gam]
(d. 1420)		(d. 1454)

William Herbert = Anne Devereux
[Earl of Pembroke]
(d. 1469)

William Herbert [Earl of Huntingdon] (d. 1491)   Walter Herbert = Anne (d. 1507)

Elizabeth Herbert = Charles Somerset
[1st Earl of Worcester]
(d. 1526)

Henry Somerset
[2nd Earl of Worcester]
(d. 1549)

William Somerset
[3rd Earl of Worcester]
(d. 1589)

Edward Somerset
[4th Earl of Worcester]
(d. 1628)

Henry Somerset
[5th Earl and 1st Marquis of Worcester]
(d. 1646)

Edward Somerset
[2nd Marquis of Worcester]
(d. 1667)

Henry Somerset
[3rd Marquis of Worcester, 1st Duke of Beaufort]
(d. 1700)

A detail of the Garter arms of William Somerset, third earl of Worcester (d. 1589), from a painting by Marcus Gheeraerts the elder, 1576 (Copyright: British Museum).

In 1468, Sir William Herbert captured Harlech Castle, the last Lancastrian stronghold in England and Wales. As a reward, the king created him earl of Pembroke.

doubt served as the administrative centre of the new Marcher lordship of Raglan, created in 1465 and independent thereafter of the lordship of Usk. Under the grant, the new lordship would be free of any interference from royal officials, and there would be a weekly market at Raglan, and a fair held twice a year in May and October. This was the only Marcher lordship created in Wales after 1284 and demonstrates further just how important William Herbert was to the king.

Herbert's final accolade came in 1468 when Edward IV created him earl of Pembroke as a reward for his capture of Harlech Castle, the last Lancastrian stronghold in England and Wales. The remarkable distinction of this honour was that Earl William had become the first member of the Welsh gentry to enter the ranks of the English peerage. His rise has been described thus: 'In less than ten years this grossly ambitious and grasping Welsh country squire had turned himself into an English magnate, with an annual income of some £2,400'.

As a consequence of his political success and the rewards which came in its wake, William Herbert was able to continue his father's work at Raglan on a grand scale. Apart from the Tudor and Jacobean rebuilding and additions, the present appearance of the castle is largely his achievement. It is not known whether the building work continued without interruption following the death of his father; possibly not. It was probably not until the early 1460s that Herbert was in a financial position to build as luxuriously as evidently he did, though some of the tiles from the refurbished chapel date to the late 1450s and the accounts from the same period record the delivery of some building materials. The work continued up to his death, for a bill dated 1469/70 refers to money brought to Raglan for the unspecified 'nywe werke' already in hand.

Earl William remodelled Raglan on a grand scale: he created a magnificent new gatehouse and approach to the castle, and developed courts on either side of the earlier great hall range to service the running of the household and to provide residential and guest accommodation.

The new gatehouse at Raglan, as elsewhere at this time, was meant to look impressive and yet it was not lacking in defensive qualities. The prominent cresting of arches or machicolations, through which missiles could be dropped on an attacker, was equally impressive as architectural display. Evidence for this form of defence can be seen elsewhere in the castle, and it was probably also a feature of the earlier Great Tower (pp. 50–51).

Visitors to the castle would have passed through the gate-passage into the Pitched Stone Court, where there was an Office Wing, kitchen and other service rooms. The Office Wing, between the Closet Tower and the Kitchen Tower, is Tudor in date, but it replaced a block built by William Herbert (pp. 32–33). The Kitchen Tower and part of the adjacent walling to the west are also Sir William's work, but the rest of the masonry is sixteenth century (including the cobbled surface, which overlies its fifteenth-century predecessor).

From here, it is likely that only guests would have taken what was in effect a processional route through one end of the fifteenth-century hall into the Fountain Court; a separate route via the pantry and buttery would have served the household staff. Around this second courtyard were arranged two blocks of sumptuous apartments, separated by a grand staircase, almost theatrical in design, providing well-appointed guest accommodation. A third suite of apartments overlooking the moat was probably reserved for residential use by the Herbert family and was accessible via a third route from the hall, behind the dais. A fourth suite of family rooms — the state apartments — also overlooked the moat and was surmounted by a conspicuous display of heraldry, with finely carved masonry shields and badges. Such displays of lineage may be seen on a number of great castles and houses of the later fourteenth and fifteenth centuries.

A chapel was built alongside the hall and a further series of well-appointed rooms occupied the upper floors of the gatehouse range and the Closet Tower.

The Great Tower — now only accessible from the most private chambers in the castle — was also remodelled. The drawbridge arrangement (pp. 49–51) was replaced by a solid bridge (itself now replaced by a modern structure) leading to a forebuilding immediately in front of the entrance to the keep. Herbert's works also included an apron wall with six turrets, built to enclose the base of the Great Tower, which obscured the earlier gunloops.

In short, William Herbert had used the remarkable wealth and power that he had amassed to build on a magnificent scale to protect, reinforce and project his own position and that of the Yorkist regime. At Raglan, he could retain a household and offer hospitality equal to that of any magnate in the land.

Fourteenth-century references to a park (p. 4) suggest that William Herbert and his father inherited a maintained landscape around the castle, and early in the 1400s mention is made of orchards bearing a wide variety of fruit. An expense account of 1457/58 refers to the garden of the lord's kitchen and in the 1490s a record is made of the wages of Ieuan Hir, bailiff, with whom lay the custody of 'the castle and the lord's garden there'. The castle and its gardens were in turn surrounded by extensive parkland, known as the Home Park. Beyond, stretching towards Llantilio Crossenny, lay the Red Deer Park, 'thick planted with oaks and several large beeches and richly stocked with deer', and referred to as 'new' in 1493, when a fence was erected around it. Both parks are marked on sixteenth- and seventeenth-century maps of Monmouthshire. A third park was known as Llantilio Park.

Amongst the few fifteenth-century references to the castle that survive in Welsh poetry is a *cywydd* by Dafydd Llwyd. He praised the castle with its 'hundred rooms filled with festive fare, its hundred chimneys for men of high degree'. In another poem, Guto'r Glyn referred to the 'fair rock-built court of Raglan'. The new earl of Pembroke was not, however, to enjoy his palatial-style castle for long. He was defeated at the battle of Edgecote in July 1469 whilst leading an army largely composed of Welshmen. Earl William and his brother, Sir Richard Herbert, were both captured. Richard Neville, earl of Warwick ('the kingmaker'), who had deserted the Yorkist cause, had them executed in Northampton the very next day, an arbitrary act, even by the standards of the time. The earl's body was brought back to south-east Wales and was buried in the Cistercian abbey church at Tintern. Patronage of the abbey had passed to him with the lordship of Chepstow in 1468.

Below left: Documents from the late fifteenth century record extensive parkland around Raglan Castle, known as the Home Park, and the Red Deer Park beyond. Both parks appear on this extract from John Speed's 1610 map of Monmouthshire.

Below right: William Herbert, earl of Pembroke, was buried in the abbey church at Tintern in 1469. Although his tomb was destroyed following the suppression of the abbey, an illustration of it appears in the family chronicle, the Herbertorum Prosapia (Cardiff Central Library, Ms. 5.7).

The join of the fifteenth-century ashlar with the Tudor sandstone, close to the Kitchen Tower, is clearly visible from the uppermost terrace at the back of the castle and may mark a hiatus in building following the death of Earl William in 1469.

William Herbert, Earl of Huntingdon, and the Later Herberts

Earl William of Pembroke's heir was his son, another William (d. 1491), by his marriage to Anne Devereux. The boy was only fourteen when his father died, and he remained a minor until 1475, Raglan remaining in the hands of his mother. She had been granted Chepstow Castle by the terms of her husband's will, and it was there that she was later to reside. The execution of his father in 1469 marked the end of the family's great influence in national affairs despite young William's marriage to Mary Woodville, sister to the queen, in 1466. In 1479, he was to suffer the indignity of being required to exchange the prestigious earldom of Pembroke — so that Edward IV could bestow it upon his own son, the prince of Wales — for the earldom of Huntingdon. Eventually, however, he became chamberlain to the prince, and under Richard III (1483–85) regained his position as chief justice of south Wales.

It is possible that there was a hiatus in major building work at Raglan following the execution of William's father in 1469. Indeed, a clear break in building, along the lines Earl William I intended, is visible from the exterior to the west of the Kitchen Tower,

marked by a change from pale finely carved or dressed stonework (ashlar) to red sandstone rubble walling. The red sandstone continuation dates to the Tudor period, but traces of the walling that marked the end of the Pitched Stone Court in the intervening period were found when the castle was being repaired in the 1950s (see plan on inside back cover). Earl William II was not in a financial position to continue the fine work of his father and it is possible that the break in the masonry represents the end of the medieval building programme. Alternatively, part of Herbert's work may have been deliberately demolished in the sixteenth century to make way for structural improvements.

Nevertheless, in spite of Earl William I's death, accounts indicate that repairs and minor building works continued at Raglan. In 1479/80 the roofs of both the hall and the chapel were tiled, and a plumber was paid 16*d*. 'for soldering and repairing the Great Tower and the chapel etc.' In 1480/81 mills and the fence of the great park were mended and a year later repairs were undertaken to 'diverse defects of the hall and great chamber on the lower side of the hall'. That domestic life at the castle also continued is demonstrated by the purchase of buckram (a fine cotton or linen fabric) and satin for the female members of the household, as well as a quantity of cloth for 'my lords lyvere', possibly for the uniforms of the staff and retainers.

William Herbert the younger, earl of Huntingdon, died in 1491 and the Herbert barony passed to his daughter, Elizabeth, there being no male heir. Raglan, however, remained for several years in the hands of the earl's younger brother, Sir Walter Herbert (d. 1507), who had been a prominent supporter of the House of York. After the landing of Henry Tudor at Milford Haven in 1485, he soon sided with the Tudor dynasty and in 1502 he entertained the king's wife at Raglan. The queen was a member of the Woodville family on her mother's side and thus had connections with Raglan, as of course did Henry VII himself (p. 9). Following Walter's death in 1507, the king granted the castle and lordship of Raglan to his widow, Anne, but when she remarried in 1508, it seems that Raglan passed to Elizabeth, the daughter of the earl of Huntingdon, and her husband, Sir Charles Somerset (d. 1526).

An inventory of the goods left by Sir Walter upon his death presumably records what was at Raglan at the time. Items listed include tapestries, bed coverings,

Like his father, Sir William Herbert, the earl of Huntingdon (d. 1491) was buried at Tintern Abbey (above) with his wife, Mary Woodville. Their tomb (right) is illustrated in the family chronicle, the Herbertorum Prosapia *(Cardiff Central Library, Ms. 5.7).*

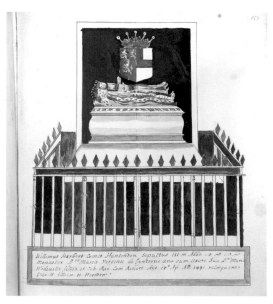

carpets, chairs and towels, as well as numerous pieces of silver plate, brass and pewter, amongst which were a pair of silver pots or flagons, each with a dragon enamelled on the top. There were also a number of fine items in the chapel (p. 41). It is very likely that the majority of these items had been at Raglan since the time of Sir William ap Thomas and his son.

The Somersets, Earls of Worcester: Tudor Rebuilding

In 1492, Elizabeth Herbert had married Sir Charles Somerset, a natural son of Henry Beaufort, duke of Somerset (d. 1464), and it is to the Somerset family that we owe the final transformation of the castle and the immediate landscape into the great Tudor country seat that Raglan became.

Sir Charles was a firm supporter of Henry VII, and became lord chamberlain to the king and to his successor, Henry VIII (1509–1547). He was prominent in the court circle and in affairs of state, and from 1504 he was styled Baron Herbert of Raglan, Chepstow and Gower, in right of his wife's inheritance. In 1513, commanding part of the royal army, he took part in Henry VIII's first military expedition to France. As a reward for his services on the campaign, the king created him earl of Worcester. Somerset died in 1526, and was buried in the Beaufort Chapel within the chapel of St George at Windsor Castle.

Sir Charles was succeeded by Henry (d. 1549), second earl of Worcester, his eldest son by his first wife, Elizabeth. He was a man with few of his father's abilities. After the suppression of the monasteries, Henry was granted various monastic properties, including the site and buildings of Tintern Abbey in 1537. In 1546 much, if not all, of the lead from the abbey was bought by the earl, presumably for building work at the castles of Raglan and Chepstow. He died three years later, and was buried in St Mary's Church, Chepstow, where his handsome tomb can still be seen.

His successors, William Somerset (d. 1589), third earl of Worcester, and his son, Edward, the fourth earl (d. 1628), were men of greater ability and ambition. Both were wealthy, brilliant and cultured men who played prominent roles at court, and it was during their time that Raglan saw its final major building phase.

Sir Charles Somerset, first earl of Worcester (d. 1526), by George Perfect Harding (d. 1853) after an unknown artist. Sir Charles succeeded to Raglan on his marriage to Elizabeth Herbert in 1492 (National Portrait Gallery, London).

The gilt-bronze tomb effigies of Henry VII (1485–1509) and his wife, Elizabeth of York (d. 1503), at Westminster Abbey. In 1462, Henry was placed in custody at Raglan where he was 'kept as prisoner, but honourably brought up with the wife of William Herbert'. Elizabeth was related to the Woodville family and in 1502 was entertained at Raglan by Sir Walter Herbert (d. 1507) (Dean and Chapter of Westminster).

The colourful tomb effigy of Henry Somerset, second earl of Worcester (d. 1549), in St Mary's Church, Chepstow.

William Somerset, third earl of Worcester

Earl William held positions at the courts of three sovereigns: Edward VI (1547–53), Mary (1553–58) and Elizabeth I (1558–1603), serving with particular distinction during the Elizabethan period. He undertook various missions abroad on behalf of the queen and was made a Knight of the Garter in 1570. Like other noblemen of his day he was a patron of the theatre, and Edward Alleyn — one of the greatest figures of the Elizabethan stage — is first heard of as a member of his company of actors. When he died in 1589 Earl William was the first of his line to be buried in Raglan Church. Little remains of his monument for it was badly damaged during the Civil War.

Earl William inherited a castle that had apparently been little altered since his Herbert ancestors had raised their monumental palace-fortress a century earlier. His work focused on improving the hall and service ranges to meet the social requirements of the day, and it can be recognized by the use of dark red sandstone as opposed to the pale yellow sandstone of the earlier period. That part of the hall which faces the Pitched Stone Court was completely rebuilt, with a fine oriel window at the upper end and a porch at the other. The hall itself was also given a new hammer-beam roof. Beyond the hall, the buildings were extended to the north, creating a new service range as far as the Kitchen Tower and it is to this time that the total rebuilding of

the Office Wing is attributed. Other buildings were heightened, including the upper storey of the gatehouse range behind the two gate towers and the private dining room in the state apartments adjoining the hall.

Perhaps the single most impressive feature was the addition of a long gallery, a feature introduced into many great Tudor houses, especially in the Elizabethan period. At Raglan this was constructed at second-floor level against the hall and buttery overlooking the Fountain Court. The fine windows at the end would have afforded a breath-taking view of the earl's magnificent new gardens and the hills beyond. Gardens were becoming grander and more spacious as Renaissance ideas were filtering through to the English court and aristocracy from France and ultimately Italy, and as a prominent and wealthy courtier, Earl William would no doubt have been keen to experiment with these Continental innovations.

We know from a plan drawn in 1652 by Laurence Smythe, and a description, written in 1674, recalling the castle and gardens as they were shortly before the Civil War siege (1646), that below the long gallery lay a series of walled terraces with formal beds. These led down to the lake, or 'great poole' as it is named on the 1652 plan, created when the Wilcae brook was dammed. Artificial lakes of this size were rare in sixteenth-century Britain, the closest parallel being perhaps the great Mere at Kenilworth Castle, Warwickshire, where the earl of Leicester staged lavish spectacles. Another water feature appears on Smythe's map: to the south, beyond the orchard and hopyard, are four rectangular islands surrounded by water, which may date from the time of Earl William or perhaps that of his son.

There was a further terrace to the south-west of the castle, and a 'garden plot, answerable in proportion to the Tower'. Well might Thomas Churchyard write in 1587 of:

The curious knots, wrought all with edged toole,
The stately Tower, that lookes ore Pond and Poole:
The Fountain trim, that runs both day and night,
Doth yeeld in showe, a rare and noble sight.

The fountain, of course, was situated in the courtyard of that name. The 'curious knots' — a Tudor speciality — were probably found in the garden plot and on the terraces. They were patterned beds of flowers, herbs or low-growing aromatic shrubs, often of intricate interwoven design.

All this work was designed to improve the accommodation and services, and reflected changes in fashion and the social requirements of an Elizabethan nobleman of Worcester's standing.

WILLIAM SOMERSET, (Son of HENRY)
3d Earl of WORCESTER.

HONI SOIT QVI MAL Y PENSE

Edward Somerset, fourth earl of Worcester

The fourth earl of Worcester, Edward, was regarded when a young man as 'the best horseman and tilter of his time', eventually receiving the prestigious royal office of Master of the Horse. He became a favourite of Queen Elizabeth I, despite his adherence to the Roman Catholic faith, so much so that she remarked of him that he reconciled what she believed impossible: 'a stiff papist to a good subject'. He remained in royal favour after the succession of James I (1603–25), serving as Earl Marshal at the coronation and as Lord Great Chamberlain when Charles I (1625–49) was crowned. Edward, like his father before him, was patron to a company of actors, and he also included in his patronage two of the greatest figures in Elizabethan music and literature, the composer William Byrd (d. 1623) and the poet Edmund Spenser (d. 1599). Byrd was Worcester's household musician, and it was in the earl's London residence, Worcester House in the Strand, that he died.

Worcester's prominent position in the late Elizabethan court is demonstrated in a remarkable picture entitled *Queen Elizabeth going in Procession to Blackfriars in 1600*, which is attributed to Robert Peake (d. 1626). Worcester stands prominently in the

Both Edward, and his successor, Henry Somerset (d. 1646), further developed the magnificent gardens at Raglan. This artist's impression shows the castle and gardens in their heyday, about 1620. The form of the gardens is based on the surviving plan of Earl Edward's garden at Worcester Lodge, Nonsuch (Illustration by Ivan Lapper, 2003).

Edward Somerset, fourth earl of Worcester (d. 1628) was prominent at the court of Elizabeth I and is shown in the foreground of this picture dressed in pink. Although this painting, attributed to Robert Peake (d. 1626), is believed to celebrate the marriage of the earl's son and heir, it may instead allude to his role as master of ceremonies and the queen's favourite. It has been suggested that the castles in the background represent the earl's castles at Chepstow (left) and Raglan (right) (By kind permission of Mr J. K. Wingfield Digby, Sherborne Castle, Dorset).

foreground with the queen, and the remaining figures are arranged about them according to their ranks and positions at court. Traditionally, the picture is thought to celebrate the marriage of the earl's heir, Henry Somerset, Lord Herbert (d. 1646), to Anne Russell. However, the painting may date to 1601, the year in which Worcester became Master of the Horse, and may allude to the earl as the queen's favourite and master of ceremonies at the Elizabethan court rather than simply depict a single event. It is interesting to note that the castles in the background may represent the earl's castles at Chepstow (left) and Raglan (right).

The building works that may be assigned with certainty to the fourth earl include the two fireplaces above the buttery, though the upper windows of the Tudor structures may also be his work. These are of traditional Elizabethan type, in stark contrast to the windows in the hall, and are of a different stone. Nevertheless, it is possible that these Bath stone, square-headed openings, including those in the long gallery, date from the 1580s and represent his father's work.

Perhaps more significantly, Earl Edward developed the magnificent gardens begun by his father. In this he may have been influenced by the grand scale and sophistication of the gardens at Nonsuch Palace, Surrey, where he was keeper of Nonsuch Great Park. At Raglan, the earl added a large formal water garden or water 'parterre' at the northern end of the great lake, with a summerhouse to one side. There was another summerhouse overlooking the terraces and no doubt the design of the gardens was simplified in keeping with the fashion of the early seventeenth century, perhaps echoing the sophisticated garden at Worcester Lodge, Nonsuch, recorded in a plan drawn by Robert Smythson in about 1609.

The earl also added the moat walk around the Great Tower, including the brick niches in the retaining wall. The niches were decorated with coloured plaster, set with patterns of shell-work, and they housed statues of Roman emperors. The appearance of such antiquities was becoming increasingly common in other contemporary great gardens and walks, no doubt inspired by the collection at

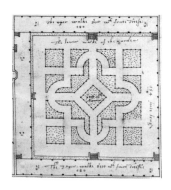

Part of the plan of Earl Edward's garden at Worcester Lodge, Nonsuch, by Robert Smythson, 1609 (RIBA Library Drawings Collection).

The remains of two of the brick summerhouses, probably built by the fourth earl, appear in this late seventeenth-century painting by Thomas Smith. The footings of that in the distance can still be seen on the upper terrace; the exact location of that shown in the foreground remains unknown, though it may be associated with the water parterre (His grace, the duke of Beaufort).

Edward Somerset's 1663 book of inventions (National Museums & Galleries of Wales).

Edward Somerset's Water Machine

A feature of the Great Tower at Raglan in the seventeenth century was an invention of Edward Somerset, Lord Herbert, later second marquis of Worcester (d.1667). He has in the past been credited with the invention of the steam engine, but it is more likely that he only experimented with steam machines. Some time between 1630 and 1640 he set up at Raglan a prototype of his 'water commanding machine'.

The mechanism was either in the keep or in the moat, although no evidence of it has ever been discovered. The apparatus was apparently capable of spouting water as high as the top of the Great Tower and was put to good effect early in the 1640s, when a group of rustics came to the castle to search for arms. Herbert's machinery was set in motion for their benefit, and upon being informed that the ensuing noise was the roar of lions, they fled empty-handed.

Arundel House, situated like Worcester House on the Strand, in London. Thomas Howard, earl of Arundel (d. 1646), and his wife had toured parts of Italy in 1613–14 in the company of the architect Inigo Jones (d. 1652), during which time they acquired many pieces of classical sculpture that were later displayed in the revolutionary new garden at Arundel House. The earl of Worcester's collection of statues of Roman emperors may well have been influenced by Arundel's acquisitions.

The gardens at Raglan were now amongst the most fashionable in the country: only royalty and a very few wealthy courtiers could aspire to such sophistication and opulence.

The end of an era

Henry, fifth earl of Worcester, inherited Raglan in 1628 and no doubt maintained his father's estate. Early in the seventeenth century the approach to the main gatehouse of the castle was enhanced, first, by the addition of the White Gate — a structure of brick and ashlar of which only a small part remains. Soon after, an outer enclosure was established in front of the White Gate, the brick footings of which now lie buried beneath the car park. A second gate, the brick-built Red Gate, was built by Earl Henry on the line of this wall and overlooked a large pool crossed by the main approach road to the castle. Although Dr Thomas Bayly describes the Red Gate as still unfinished at the outset of the Civil War in 1642, a late seventeenth-century painting by Thomas Smith depicts the gate standing to a considerable height (p. 56).

In the years leading up to the Civil War, Raglan was at its zenith and a vivid picture of the castle and gardens at this time is recorded in a description written in 1674. Pride of place is given to the Great Tower and surrounding moat, in which stood the 'rare artificial water work' — a powerful fountain. There is also a record of the many rooms in the castle and a fascinating account of the ritual involved in serving dinner to the earl, his family and friends, and his household staff (p. 36–37). But within a decade, all of this would come to an end following the defeat of King Charles I, for whom Earl Henry declared his unswerving support in the summer of 1642.

Raglan and the Civil War

Oxford Garrison having run to its period of obstinacy against the Parliament, and being now reduced, many other Garrisons that attended its fate fell with it, even like ripe fruit, with an easie touch: But these two Garrisons of Ragland and Pendennis, like winter fruit, hung long on.
Joshua Sprigge, *Anglia Rediviva* (1647)

The defeat of the royalist army at the battle of Naseby in June 1645 had virtually sealed the military fate of King Charles I. The war continued until 1646, although only a few isolated pockets of royalist resistance were left, and eventually they too fell. Pendennis in Cornwall surrendered on 16 August 1646, and Raglan followed suit three days later. The first Civil War had ended. Only Harlech Castle held out for longer, until March 1647.

Henry, earl of Worcester, was a staunch royalist and held Raglan Castle for the king, by whom he had been created marquis of Worcester in 1643. It was said that the marquis personally supported the garrison of the castle financially to the sum of £40,000. According to Joshua Sprigge, the garrison consisted of 800 people in 1646, both horse and foot, together with civilians. Besides this outlay, the marquis is reputed to have contributed almost £1,000,000 to the royal cause, and on more than one occasion during the war King Charles was entertained at Raglan. The royalist, Richard Symonds (d. 1660), who has left us an account of some of the Civil War campaigning, stated that the marquis's estate was 'esteemed 24 thowsand pounds per annum'. Symonds also mentioned that in 1645 there were 300 infantryman at Raglan, all 'constantly paid'.

The provision of more-up-to-date defences to enable the castle to withstand a siege was essential. New fortifications in Europe were being built lower than medieval castles to make them less vulnerable to artillery fire. But the key to the new system was the angle bastion, an arrow-shaped gun platform which allowed ordnance to flank the ground in front of the defences between two bastions. Therefore, earthworks, possibly with timber and wicker breastworks, were built out in front of the castle. These probably utilized the line of the outer enclosure, and incorporated the area now occupied by the later seventeenth-century farmhouse as well as the present farm buildings.

Henry Somerset, first marquis of Worcester (d. 1646), seen here in this portrait by or after C. Johnson, was a staunch royalist and held Raglan for the king during the siege of 1646 (His grace, the duke of Beaufort).

King Charles I (1625–49) was entertained at Raglan by the marquis of Worcester several times during the course of the Civil War. This triple portrait of the king, by Sir Anthony van Dyck (d. 1641), was painted around 1636–37 (The Royal Collection © 2003, Her Majesty Queen Elizabeth II).

Above: Traces of the Civil War earthworks at Raglan can still be seen. This aerial view shows the royalist artillery bastion close to the castle at A, with the parliamentarian battery point at B (Cambridge University Collection: copyright reserved, AZR-40).

Right: An illustration of 1650 showing a mortar in use. Mortars were designed to fire iron spheres filled with gunpowder. The powder was ignited by a slow-burning fuse, ideally on impact with the target.

This extension of Raglan's defences made it possible for the large garrison to mount an effective defence with heavy ordnance on the bastions, and lighter cannon positioned on the towers of the castle. The guns on the bastions were probably mounted on wooden platforms behind earth-filled wicker baskets or gabions. One bastion lies at the entrance to the present car park, mainly in the adjacent field [**A**], and the remains of other earthworks lie in the trees on the far side of the farmyard. The remains of the parliamentarian siegeworks survive on the high ground beyond the farm [**B**]. This battery — in which there is now a modern water tank — together with the bastion, can be seen from the top of the Great Tower. It was from the direction of the parliamentarian battery that most damage was inflicted on the castle during the siege.

Following the surrender of Raglan to parliamentarian forces in August 1646, the elderly marquis was taken prisoner and transported to London, together with his doctor and servants, but he died shortly afterwards in December of the same year. He was, however, accorded a state burial, albeit according to the rites of the Presbyterian church, and was interred in the Beaufort Chapel at Windsor Castle.

Deliberate destruction of Raglan Castle added to the damage already sustained during the siege. It doubtless encompassed the loss of the great library of books and manuscripts collected since the fifteenth century, reputedly including a fine collection of Welsh documents. One account, written in 1674, records the memory of the slighting of Raglan: *Afterwards it [the castle] was demolished, the lead & timber carried to Monmouth there by water to rebuild Bristoll bridg after the last fire, & the woods in ye 3 parkes destroyed. The tower Mellin was undermined & supported with timber till 2 sid[e]s of 6 were cut through; the timber being burnt it fel downe in a lump & soe rema[i]ns. After ye surrender the country people were sommoned as to a Randevow with spads & pixaxes to draw ye mote in hope of treasure; that failing they were sett to cut the stanks [banks or dams] of the great fishpond, where was great store of carpe & other fish. The artificial roofe of the hall could not safely be taken downe, remained above 20 yeares till it perish by ye weather. There remaines about 30 valts of cellers, bridgis and other roomes at present. The large valt of the tower bridg & most curious arches of the chappell with many valts more [are] totally destroyed.*

The Siege of Raglan, 1646

Joshua Sprigge (d. 1684), chaplain to Sir Thomas Fairfax (d. 1671), commander-in-chief of the parliamentarian forces, the New Model Army, wrote a vivid account of the siege and capture of Raglan in his book *Anglia Rediviva*. During June and July 1646, Colonel Thomas Morgan (d. 1679), a fine and experienced soldier, had been besieging the castle, but it still held out, refusing all summonses to surrender. Morgan had with him Captain John Hooper, an engineer, and at the end of July, Hooper had built a battery from which the guns had put out of action a number of cannon mounted on the towers of the castle; several cannon balls have been discovered embedded in parts of the castle walls.

Some idea of the size of the garrison defending the castle is given in a letter dated 23 July from Colonel Morgan to the Speaker of the House of Commons. Morgan mentions that earlier that month eighty cavalry and four hundred infantry sallied out against his forces. Before they were repulsed, Morgan lost an ensign and two infantry, the royalists suffering two captains killed and an unspecified number of other men.

Fairfax himself arrived at Raglan in August, and Sprigge mentions that the siegeworks dug by the parliamentarians were slowly approaching the defences which had been erected around the castle. When Hooper was within sixty yards of the defenders he 'planted' mortar batteries, one of the mortars, 'Roaring Meg', being brought down by Colonel John Birch, governor of Hereford. On 14 August new approach works were started, and the marquis, realizing that further resistance was futile, sued for surrender.

The formal surrender took place on 19 August, once the surrender document consisting of six articles had been agreed by both sides. The marquis, waiting in the hall, together with his household, 'could see through the window the General [Fairfax] with all his officers entering the Outward Court, as if a floodgate had been left open'. The garrison was permitted to march away 'with their Horses and Armes, with Colours flying, Drums beating, Trumpet sounding', except for those exempted from pardon, and the sick and the wounded also remained behind.

Amongst the munitions found in the castle were twenty guns, but only one barrel of gunpowder. However, the garrison had made a mill within the defences which could make a barrel of powder a day. It is not known how many casualties the two sides suffered, but there is a memorial in Gloucester Cathedral, defaced after the Restoration, to William White who was killed at the siege of Raglan.

Left: Sir Thomas Fairfax (d. 1671), commander-in-chief of the New Model Army, from an engraving published in 1647. Sir Thomas's deployment of mortars during his supervision of the closing stages of the siege of Raglan may well have encouraged the marquis to surrender (National Portrait Gallery, London).

Above: Part of a Civil War period cannon shot mould found at Raglan Castle. It is the bottom half of a two-part mould; the upper section would have contained the hole through which the molten iron was poured. The mould would have produced 3 inch (7.6cm) diameter cannon balls, suitable for the small guns that the royalists mounted on the towers of the castle.

Left: 'Roaring Meg', a mortar that may have been used at the siege of Raglan and now at Hereford. The bed on which it rests, however, is modern.

From the Civil War to the Present Day

Above: Part of the carved oak frieze, now at Cefntilla, which probably came from Raglan. The heraldry and initials, EW, may refer to Elizabeth Worcester, which would date the frieze to about 1514 (Centre for Advanced Welsh and Celtic Studies, Aberystwyth: Martin Crampin).

Below: In 1660, Henry Somerset, third marquis of Worcester (d. 1700), began to rebuild Badminton House, Gloucestershire, which remains the Somerset family home today (His grace, the duke of Beaufort).

Below right: An elaborately carved chimney-piece at Badminton House, which may have come from the parlour at Raglan and serves as a reminder of the castle's once sumptuous rooms (His grace, the duke of Beaufort).

The castle and other property were confiscated after the siege, with the lordship of Chepstow being granted to Oliver Cromwell (d. 1658) himself. The grandson of the first marquis, Henry Somerset, third marquis of Worcester from 1667 (d. 1700), was able to recover much of the former possessions of the family, including the castle, before the end of the Commonwealth. The family still owned the Tudor mansion, Troy House, just outside Monmouth, but after the restoration of King Charles II (1660–85) in 1660, the third marquis began to rebuild Badminton House in Gloucestershire, the fourth earl having bought the manor in 1608. He also largely rebuilt Troy House in the 1680s as the Monmouthshire seat of his son and heir. The marquis built Great Castle House in Monmouth, completed in 1673, following his appointment as Lord President

of the Council of Wales and the Marches the year before. Any thoughts that there may have been of rebuilding Raglan were certainly abandoned by or soon after the Restoration, but the village church remained a place of burial for the family as late as 1710. Since 1682, when Henry, the third marquis, was created a duke, the family has borne the title of dukes of Beaufort.

In common with other castles, Raglan was used as a convenient source of building material in the late seventeenth and eighteenth centuries. The Somersets had obviously been able to salvage some of their belongings in 1646 and later, for there is at Badminton House a portrait of William, third earl of Worcester, which is thought to have hung at Raglan. There is also a carved wooden chimney-piece at Badminton, removed from Troy House, Monmouth, in 1895, which is believed to have once been at Raglan, and at nearby Cefntilla there is a carved oak frieze that may have come from Raglan, possibly from the parlour. The heraldry and the initials, EW, may refer to Elizabeth Worcester, which would date the frieze to about 1514, the year in which

By the beginning of the nineteenth century, ivy-clad Raglan had become a tourist attraction. This view shows the back of the gatehouse from the Pitched Stone Court in about 1850.

Henry Somerset, fifth duke of Beaufort (d. 1803), who put an end to the despoliation of Raglan in the mid-eighteenth century (His grace, the duke of Beaufort).

her husband, Charles, was created first earl of Worcester (p. 13). Perhaps removed from the castle during the Civil War, the frieze was recorded at Raglan by the Revd John Skinner in 1832, where it had been re-erected in the great hall by the duke of Beaufort in the 1820s for a 'Grand Entertainment'. The great hall had been reroofed for the occasion.

But already, in the first half of the eighteenth century, one Hopkins, an estate surveyor of the Beauforts, had earned for himself the title of 'Grand Dilapidator' as a result of the removal of the chimney-pieces and window frames. He had also overseen the removal of twenty-three staircases. Fortunately, the succession of Henry Somerset, fifth duke of Beaufort (d. 1803), in 1756 brought an end to these depredations.

Thereafter the ivy-clad ruin became a romantic attraction complete with rustic bridges, seats and fences as well as its own guidebook, which by 1829 was in its eleventh edition. Minor repairs were undertaken during the ensuing years, and the walls were slowly freed from vegetation. In 1938 Raglan was placed in the guardianship of the Commissioners of HM Works by the tenth duke of Beaufort, and in the twenty years following the end of World War II an extensive programme of conservation was carried out. The castle is now maintained by Cadw on behalf of the National Assembly for Wales.

A Tour of Raglan Castle

The tour suggests one route through the castle. It follows the progress that a distinguished visitor or family member might have made from the main gatehouse via the service areas — the Pitched Stone Court — used by the entire household, through the hall range to the lavish guest accommodation in the Fountain Court, and thence to the most private chambers reserved for the lord of Raglan, from where access is gained to the Great Tower. From here you are invited to explore the gardens and view the magnificent surrounding landscape in which the earls of Worcester created a fabulous Renaissance garden. Aside from this tour, visitors may investigate the various parts of the castle in any order, using the bird's-eye view (inside front cover) or the ground plan (inside back cover) as a guide.

Before entering the gatehouse, it is worth pausing to look at the exterior of this splendid palace-fortress. In front of you is the gatehouse range — one of the most imposing frontages of the later Middle Ages, built with the fine ashlar masonry used throughout the fifteenth-century castle.

To the right is the Closet Tower, which provided comfortable and secure accommodation, and to the left of the gatehouse are the remains of the magnificent state apartments overlooking the moat, distinguished by their large windows decorated with carved heraldic panels. These chambers were almost certainly reserved for the lord of Raglan, along with the Great Tower which sits isolated outside the main curtain wall. This massive, gently tapering tower dominates the whole approach to the castle and is a reminder that defensive considerations were not neglected at Raglan. The whole ensemble was built in no more than fifty years with a unity of design that is given emphasis by the fine stonework and prominent machicolated battlements. No one arriving at Raglan in the time of Sir William Herbert could fail to be impressed by this very public display of wealth, power and status.

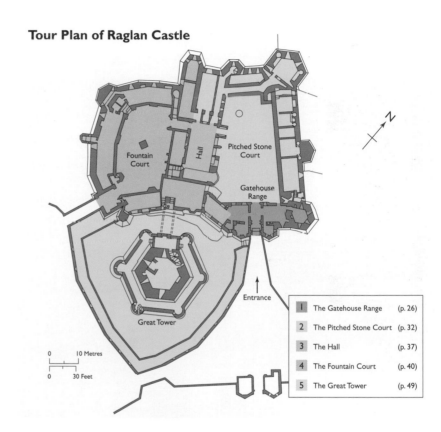

Tour Plan of Raglan Castle

Fountain Court

Hall

Pitched Stone Court

Gatehouse Range

Entrance

Great Tower

| 0 | 10 Metres |
| 0 | 30 Feet |

1	The Gatehouse Range	(p. 26)
2	The Pitched Stone Court	(p. 32)
3	The Hall	(p. 37)
4	The Fountain Court	(p. 40)
5	The Great Tower	(p. 49)

Left: One of the gargoyles on the gate-tower machicolations.

Opposite: Sir William Herbert's magnificent gatehouse range was built both to impress and to intimidate visitors arriving at Raglan, and from the 1460s served as the main entrance to the castle.

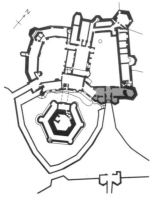

The Gatehouse Range

The gatehouse range is considered in three parts: the gatehouse itself, which consists of two half-hexagonal towers on either side of a gate-passage; rooms on each side of, and above, the gate-passage at the back of the gatehouse; and the adjacent Closet Tower.

Exterior

The approach to the great gate is over a two-arched bridge, an arrangement dating from the sixteenth century, but partly restored in 1949. These arches replaced the medieval drawbridge that crossed the ditch in front of the gate, which, when raised, would have fitted within the rectangular recess of the outermost arch.

The gatehouse itself consists of an entrance passage with rooms in the two half-hexagonal towers

at four levels, from the basement through to the second floor, with battlements and wall-walks above. The upper rooms were probably occupied by the chief official or constable, who would have had charge of Raglan in the absence of the lord of the castle. In the angle against the south-west (left) tower there is a latrine serving the gatehouse and the adjacent state apartments. The latrine chute terminates in an arched opening at the level of the moat.

The circular openings beneath the ground-floor windows of the gatehouse and the adjacent buildings are gunloops of a type common in the fifteenth century; further examples can be seen throughout the castle, often set at more than one level. Many were built within latrines and fireplaces and could not have been very effective, perhaps indicating that their chief purpose was to look impressive from the outside.

The gatehouse was also defended by machicolations (a series of arched openings at battlement level), through which suitable missiles could be dropped on a besieging enemy, or water poured down on any fires lit against the gate. Equally, they added a sense of grandeur to the whole castle and this may have been their main purpose. The outer doorway of the gate-passage was equipped with its own machicolations at a lower level, the remains of which can be seen on each of the flanking towers. Below them are indications of the cusped windows lighting the room above the gate-passage. On the tower machicolations, note the gargoyles, alternate ones originally serving as rainwater spouts.

The Passage

The gateway of any castle was its most vulnerable point. At Raglan, beyond the gunloops, machicolations and ditch crossed by the drawbridge, access to the Pitched Stone Court was controlled by five more barriers in the gate-passage. First, there was a portcullis, then a two-leaved timber door, a second portcullis, and, finally, two more double doors (see reconstruction drawing, p. 28).

Small circular holes on either side of the entrance to the gatehouse may have acted as spy-holes or as openings for handguns. Below the bridge is the pit into which the rear portion of the drawbridge sank

when it was in the 'up' position. Immediately inside the entrance are the vertical grooves for the outer portcullis, which run up to just below the machicolations of the gate towers. Both portcullises would seem to have been worked from the room above the gate-passage, although capable of being raised to the upper level. The small holes in the grooves of the outer portcullis may also be gunloops or spy-holes, for use when the portcullis was raised. To the right, running into the drawbridge pit, is a drain from the porter's lodge in the north-east tower. Just beyond the outer portcullis are the jambs for the outer double doors that would have opened inwards.

Opposite: The prominent machicolations on the gatehouse range give the castle a distinctly French appearance. Both William Herbert and his father had served in France and this may have influenced their work at Raglan.

Left: The elaborate machicolations on the gatehouse of the castle of La Ferté-Milon, Aisne. The imposing façade bears a striking resemblance to the gatehouse at Raglan, which may have been inspired by such designs (Richard Avent).

The base of a latrine chute, which served the gatehouse and adjoining state apartments. Above the chute and arrowloop is an impressive array of circular gunloops. Some of these gunloops were constructed in positions where they could not have been used effectively and may have been built for display rather than defence.

Evidence in the side walls of the gate-passage for a vaulted roof above.

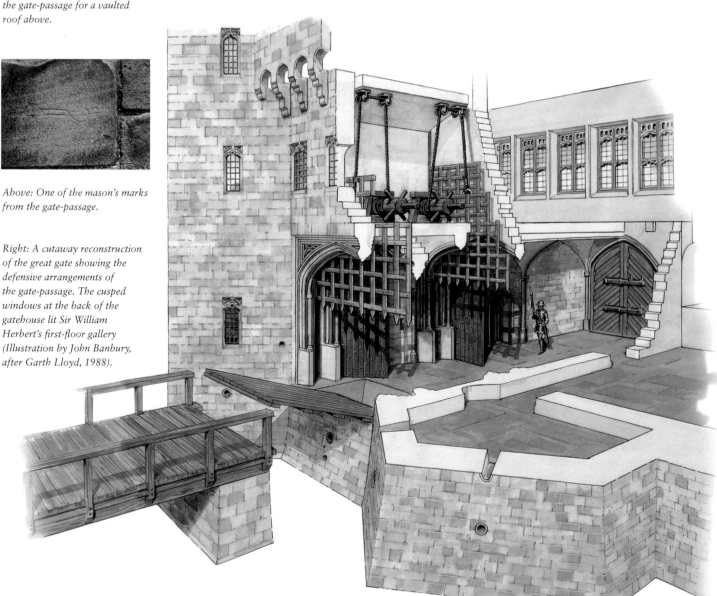

Above: One of the mason's marks from the gate-passage.

Right: A cutaway reconstruction of the great gate showing the defensive arrangements of the gate-passage. The cusped windows at the back of the gatehouse lit Sir William Herbert's first-floor gallery (Illustration by John Banbury, after Garth Lloyd, 1988).

The entrance passage leads past two small windows in the porters' lodges, past the grooves of the inner portcullis, and so on to two more doorways. Two further details are worthy of attention. First, there is evidence in the side walls for the vaulting which covered the passage. This consists of one bay in the outer section between the portcullises, and two bays beyond. Second, the walls are notable for the number and variety of masons' marks, especially round the door of the antechamber on the left.

The South-West (Left) Side

Doorways on each side of the gate-passage lead into antechambers, now both roofless.

In the Tudor period, increased space was provided in the gatehouse range by the addition of an attic. Originally, one room occupied the greater part of the first floor of the entire gatehouse range. Access to this upper floor was from the newel staircase in the far corner of this antechamber — the remains of the first-floor door off the stair can be seen — and probably from the adjacent state apartments. The range of large windows overlooking the courtyard indicates the extent of this first-floor room, and it is likely that it was the principal gallery of the castle until the third earl of Worcester built the long gallery (pp. 42–43). Sir William Herbert's gallery, which may have housed the library, is now subdivided by a later cross-wall that towers above the gate-passage. This wall is pierced by a doorway, and has a Tudor fireplace on either side; the fireplace at the higher level is a Gothic imitation of about 1810. The outline of the attic roof can be seen just below the chimney and the sockets for the joists, which supported the attic floor, are visible in the walls of the partition.

In the antechamber itself, on the immediate left on entering, a door leads into a porter's lodge (which now houses an exhibition). Beyond, there is a modern doorway to the latrine block, which now has a solid earthen floor, and contains two gunloops. Just past this doorway, a series of stone toothing projects from the wall, marking the site of the cross-wall which divided the antechamber from the state apartments. On the courtyard side of the chamber, what appears to be a damaged doorway originally served as a window.

North-East (Right) Side

On the opposite side of the gate-passage, the door into the other antechamber has undergone considerable alteration, with a wide arch no doubt dating to the renovations of the nineteenth century. The brick fireplace and oven in the chamber are also of that period, part of the lodgings for the caretaker who looked after the castle at this time. There are three original fifteenth-century doorways in this room. The one on the extreme right leads into the stone-vaulted porter's lodge. The openings in this room, just above floor level, are the gunloops. These loops were designed for small iron breech-loaders mounted on wooden beds, but they would have been difficult to aim or traverse as there were no sighting slits, merely the windows above. The effectiveness of such openings is questionable; the defence of the castle is more likely to have depended upon the garrison on the battlements and elsewhere.

The remains of the newel staircase in the south-west antechamber that led to the first floor of the gatehouse. No other traces of a stair connecting the two floors survive.

Left: The sixteenth-century cross-wall, inserted above the gate-passage, divided the first-floor gallery and created a second floor with attic space above. Both floors were given new Tudor fireplaces.

Above: The wide entrance arch into the north-east antechamber, which probably results from nineteenth-century renovation work.

Opposite: The impressive first-floor windows of Sir William Herbert's gallery dominate the rear façade of the gatehouse range, overlooking the Pitched Stone Court. To the left is the Closet Tower and to the right, part of the hall range.

Below: The Closet Tower was built as an integral part of the gatehouse range but all three floors above basement level were independent of the others, with separate access arrangements, suggesting that each floor had a distinct purpose.

The Closet Tower

There are two ground-floor doors into the Closet Tower. That on the right led to a flight of stairs down through a further doorway into the basement, which may have served as the castle's prison. Its only light and ventilation came from a long, narrow shaft descending from a slender window. The doors at the top and the bottom of the stairs were subsequently widened, perhaps to allow the use of the cellar for storing casks and barrels. But, equally, it is possible that the alterations date from the 1640s, and that the basement was used as the magazine during the Civil War. The thick walls and vaulted ceiling would have provided strong protection against cannon and plunging mortar fire.

The door on the left leads into the ground floor of the Closet Tower. This well-lit room has a latrine and a fireplace, although the latter was altered in the nineteenth century. There are gunloops below the windows. The room above (not currently accessible), like the gallery in the gatehouse range, could only be accessed by the newel stair in the south-west antechamber.

At the top of the tower, the second floor consists of a small square room with a fireplace and four small windows. It was entered through doors off the battlemented wall-walk, between the tower and the gatehouse, and from the fifteenth-century Office Wing, and this may have been the original treasury or the muniment room. It is interesting to note that each of the three floors was independent of the others and had its own separate access arrangements.

The Courtyard Side of the Gatehouse

Although badly damaged, the remarkable quality of the decoration of the first-floor windows, which lit the fifteenth-century gallery, emphasizes the importance of the domestic aspects of the gatehouse range. It is evident that the two windows on the ground floor to the right were also the work of skilled craftsmen, but all that remains are the tips of the pinnacled shafts of one window. The windows in the top floor lit the attic rooms that were added in the sixteenth century.

There have obviously been structural problems in the right-hand corner, as indicated by the misshapen window on the top floor. Much of the patching work at ground level may be the result of strengthening the wall. The brick buttressing partially obscures the fifteenth-century door into the basement, originally reached by a timber staircase. The carved figures in the wall above the basement door may be late medieval features, though they could be insertions of the last century.

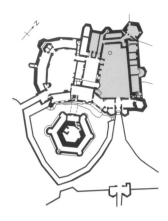

The Pitched Stone Court

The Pitched Stone Court was principally the domain of the household staff, who would have lodged in accommodation in the upper floors of the now largely ruined Office Wing, Kitchen Tower and pantry range, which occupy two sides of the court. The ground-floor rooms and cellars were all utilized in the provision and preparation of foodstuffs for the Herbert and Somerset households.

To the west (left) lies the hall range, which divides the castle in two, both physically and in terms of status, and it is to here that family and guests would have progressed from the gatehouse during the fifteenth century and later.

The cobbling is contemporary with the Tudor remodelling of the castle as are the drainage channels, which were intended to take rainwater from the lead spouts that would have projected from the surrounding buildings, but the original fifteenth-century pitching lies some 15 inches (0.4m) beneath. One other feature of the court is the well at the lower end.

The Pitched Stone Court — so named because of its cobbled surface — contained the service rooms and accommodation for the household staff. Although the present arrangement dates mainly from the Tudor remodelling of Raglan, remains of the fifteenth-century buildings were recorded during clearance and consolidation of the castle.

The Office Wing

This wing runs down the north-eastern side of the court, and it is a Tudor replacement of the original fifteenth-century range. The foundations of Sir William Herbert's earlier wing are, however, known from excavation (see plan inside back cover), and evidence of this can be seen in the rough stonework to the right of the first-floor window of the Closet Tower.

The ground-floor and first-floor windows of the Closet Tower, now situated within the line of the Tudor Office Wing, initially lay outside the fifteenth-century wall. The brick patching below the upper window marks the site of the latrine, which was replaced in the sixteenth century by a staircase connecting the Closet Tower to the new Office Wing. A flight of steps and a passage, enclosing a latrine, lead down past the sloping plinth of the tower to a small postern or back door. This enabled supplies to be brought directly into the kitchens, and may have provided access to the stables outside.

The room nearest the Closet Tower, with a drain running through the outer wall, was possibly the brewhouse. The rooms on the upper floors were probably damaged in the siege of 1646, for it was this side of the castle that bore the brunt of the

artillery bombardment. Beyond the brewhouse is a bakehouse containing a fireplace flanked by ovens. The fireplace would have provided the hot ashes used to heat the ovens in readiness for baking. There is no evidence for the chimney of the fireplace, only three draught holes in the wall behind. The outer facings of these holes are reused gunloops, presumably from the destroyed fifteenth-century curtain wall. Two rooms lay above this bakehouse, providing accommodation for household staff.

The remaining rooms in the Office Wing contained more fireplaces and ovens, with chambers above. Although the exact purpose of these rooms cannot be identified with certainty, it is clear that the new range afforded improved service facilities as well as staff accommodation, commensurate with the requirements of a great household (see p. 36).

The Kitchen Tower

At the end of the Office Wing stands the impressive fifteenth-century hexagonal Kitchen Tower. In the corner adjacent to the Office Wing, there is a cross-slit in the upper part of the tower, lighting a mural passage, and a blocked window can be seen below. Like the windows in the Closet Tower mentioned above, these originally lay outside the line of the earlier curtain wall. A stair, of which all but the foundation has disappeared, led from the adjacent corner of the courtyard to the upper floors of the Office Wing and the pantry. From this stair a door led in to the mural passage and up to the first floor of the tower.

The door below leads to a flight of steps down into the basement of the tower. This was the Wet Larder, so named in a document of 1674, and may have been used as a store for fish, meat, cheese and other dairy products. The stone-vaulted basement is a cold room, even in a hot summer.

The entrance to the kitchen itself is on the ground floor. Access is by way of a wide arch and a triangular vestibule, originally lit by two narrow windows, one of which was blocked in the sixteenth century. To the right of the kitchen door is a servery hatch. Two large fireplaces dominate the kitchen, each with an oven, and drains are still visible in two corners and below a window.

The stone vault over the kitchen has virtually disappeared, revealing that the first floor was divided

This illustration from the 1598 Ordinances of the York Baker's Company depicts various stages in the preparation of bread. Such scenes are likely to have been familiar in the sixteenth-century bakehouse at Raglan (British Library, Additional Ms. 34605, f. 25).

Part of the Office Wing, which forms the eastern perimeter of the castle and contains a series of rooms with fireplaces and ovens that were probably used for baking and brewing. It was this area of the castle that bore the brunt of the parliamentarian assault of 1646.

One of the two large fireplaces used for cooking in the Kitchen Tower. A drain is visible beneath the window to the left of the fireplace.

A woodcut illustration of a Tudor kitchen in about 1581 (English Heritage).

Right: One of the chambers above the kitchen, equipped with an ornate fireplace and windows with seats, was probably occupied by a household officer of some consequence — perhaps the clerk of the kitchen.

Below: Only the outer wall of the pantry range (centre) now survives. It was from the pantry, located on the ground floor, that bread and salt were allocated to the household.

into two rooms. The outer room — the more private of the two — has an ornate fireplace set between a pair of windows with seats in the embrasures. It was clearly a chamber for a person of some consequence in the household — perhaps the clerk of the kitchen — in spite of being situated above the kitchen. The inner room also had a fireplace, and was lit by a three-light window and a single light. From one corner, a short flight of steps passes up through the thickness of the wall to the original machicolated battlements, later destroyed in the 1646 siege, whilst from the other corner a passage runs along the top of the pantry range.

The north-east exterior face of this tower has at some stage been largely refaced in brick, perhaps in the nineteenth century. With an indication of a chimney at the top of the facing, it seems that this building served some agricultural or industrial purpose. It is not clear whether or not this refacing is associated with the stone ramp to the east of the tower.

The Pantry

The pantry lies on the north-west side of the court, but only the outer wall remains standing. The foundations of the inner wall are on the courtyard side of what is now an open path (originally a passage) linking the Kitchen Tower to the buttery in the hall range. The pantry itself was on the ground floor, lit by three cusped windows. This was the province of the pantler, the household official responsible for the allocation of bread, salt and other pantry items. A timber staircase would have given access to the necessary storage area in the cellar below. There were two storeys above the pantry and the original positions of the floors are indicated by the doors and the grooves and sockets in the walls. The chambers contained herein presumably provided more accommodation for the household staff.

The pantry is Tudor in date, except for the narrow trefoil window and the fireplace close to the Kitchen Tower. These features indicate that Sir William Herbert did plan a range in the same position, as does the line of the low-pitched roof that can be seen at the top of the Kitchen Tower. His execution in 1469 may have brought about a halt in the building programme, and a break in the masonry — visible from the exterior — may mark this hiatus (p. 12).

The Buttery

The passage that ran in front of the pantry range led into the buttery, which occupied the lower end of the hall range. From this room ale and perhaps cider were usually dispensed to the household; so was wine, which is likely to have been reserved for the lord of Raglan, his family and guests.

On entering the buttery block, low foundations running along the length of the building can be seen. These represent a wall that divided the buttery itself from a narrower passage, which connected the kitchen on the outer side of the courtyard with the hall, and led to a stair in the turret to the right. The stair led to the upper chambers, though the steps have long since been removed leaving a scar which spirals up the wall, presumably the work of the Grand Dilapidator (p. 23). However, the steps to the basement remain, leading to a passage which opens into a room that may have been used to store ale or wine.

Of the three doors in the end wall of the buttery, that on the left led from the passage into the hall via a small vestibule; the door in the centre led to a servery hatch, separated by walls from the vestibules on either side; and the door on the right led into the hall.

The buttery was originally a shorter building, about half its present length, and was two storeyed. The foundations of the original outer wall, which continued the line of the Fountain Court curtain, exist below the present floor level (see plan on inside back cover). The extension of the range outwards, and the addition of a second floor, date from the sixteenth-century rebuilding. The buttery itself was a low room lit by a three-light window.

The first floor consisted of two rooms, each with a fireplace and served by a latrine. The uppermost floor also had two rooms with more ornate fireplaces of late Elizabethan or early Jacobean date. The door in the outer room led to the long gallery. These upper rooms below — or beyond — the hall were well-appointed chambers designed for important household staff who required access to the rooms occupied by the Somersets.

The hall range contained two separate chambers at ground level: the hall itself (left), entered via a three storey porch directly from the Pitched Stone Court, and the buttery (right), which was entered from a passage that connected with the kitchen. It was from the buttery that beer, cider or wine, as appropriate, would be dispensed to members of the household.

Opposite: Few illustrations of
household dining arrangements
in Britain survive from the
late sixteenth and seventeenth
centuries. However, this
anonymous picture, after Hans
Holbein (d. 1543), of Henry VIII
(1509–1547) dining alone gives
some indication of the ritualistic
arrangements that the earls of
Worcester seem to have observed
until the 1640s (Copyright:
British Museum).

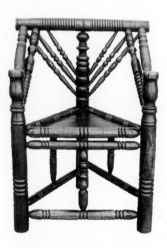

*Above: One of a set of late
sixteenth- or early seventeenth-
century chairs believed to have
been used in the hall at Raglan
(National Museums & Galleries
of Wales).*

*Right: The High Great Chamber
at Hardwick Hall, Derbyshire,
is one of the grandest rooms to
survive from the end of Elizabeth
I's reign. The private apartments
reserved for the lord of Raglan
and his guests may well have
been decorated on a similarly
lavish scale (National Trust
Photographic Library: Andreas
von Einsiedel).*

The Great Household

*At eleven o'clock the Castle Gates were shut,
and the Tables laid; Two in the Dining-Room;
Three in the Hall; One in Mrs Watson's
Apartment, where the Chaplains eat …
Two in the House-keeper's Room, for Women.*

*The Earl came into the Dining-Room, attended
by his Gentlemen … At the first Table sate
the noble Family, and such of the Nobility as
came there.*

*At the second Table … sate Knights and
honourable Gentlemen…*

*In the Hall, at the first Table sate Sir Ralph
Blackstone, Steward. The Comptroller …
Master of the Horse … Master of the Fish-ponds
… With such Gentlemen as came there under
the degree of a knight …*

*At the second Table … sate the Sewer, with
the Gentlemen Waiters, and Pages, to the
Number of twenty-four.*

*At the third Table … sate the Clerk of the
Kitchen, with the Yeoman Officers of the House,
two Grooms of the Chambers …*

This remarkable record of the dining
arrangements at Raglan in the 1640s not only
provides a valuable insight into the composition of a
great household but also its hierarchic structure and
the ritualistic way in which dining was conducted.
The earl of Worcester and his guests ate in the
privacy of the dining room and the remainder of the
household used the hall, where the steward, Sir Ralph
Blackstone, presided over the head officer's table.
The occupants of the remaining tables were ranked
according to their status: the sewer was in charge of
the dining arrangements in the hall and the serving of
the food. The clerk of the kitchen was responsible
for the purchase and provision of food and oversaw
the yeoman officers who would have had charge of
the running of different aspects of the household,
such as the cellars, pantry and buttery, and so forth.
Footmen, grooms and menial servants would have
swelled the ranks further and, although the exact
complement would vary at any time, the household
would have numbered close to 150, the majority of
whom would have been male.

Such arrangements appear to have had a long
ancestry and may have differed little from those at the
Herbert castle and the Bloet manor house. The great
household was after all the lifeblood of Raglan — the
building itself was no more than a stage occupied by
what was often a peripatetic household that arrived

complete with furnishings, pots and pans and every other accoutrement to make the empty chambers comfortable. Indeed, a 1643 inventory of Worcester House in The Strand, London, reveals a comfortably equipped house. Mrs Watson's chamber, for example, had four pieces of tapestry, and a down bed with feather bolster, pillow, quilt and two blankets.

The household itself would have consisted of the lord, his family and the close group of attendants that surrounded him — and those that served the needs of this distinguished group: cooks, scullions, household officials and all manner of other servants. Retainers might also be called upon to supplement the household at times of extra need. Together, this large and highly organized group of people would have served to perpetuate the power and prestige of their lord.

Although the seventeenth-century description records some of the names and offices of the Worcester household, few records of the Bloet family survive, though we know that the administrator of the manor of Raglan, the reeve, lived in a first-floor chamber in the fourteenth-century manor house. Fifteenth-century records, however, mention a number of names and offices: Roger Bromfield was both chaplain and steward of the household in the 1450s and 1460s; John Cook was keeper of the household in 1465/66; and in the 1470s and 1480s Adam ap Meuric was recorded in an accounting role. There is also reference in the 1450s to a butler, cook and scullion, perhaps indicating that the roles and responsibilities of the household differed little over the centuries.

The Hall

Returning to the Pitched Stone Court, we can now continue the route taken by guests to the castle in the later Middle Ages. For the Herberts, Somersets and guests alike, the hall effectively provided the main entrance to the apartments arranged around the Fountain Court. By the middle of the fifteenth century, the hall had become the centre for ceremonial occasions rather than for everyday dining and, more often, family and guests would eat elsewhere in greater privacy, leaving the hall for many of the household staff to eat their meals.

Before entering the hall itself, note the fine Tudor oriel window lighting the dais end of the hall and the grand porch. The remaining features of the hall frontage also date from the time of the reconstruction of the building by the third earl of Worcester, though the lower courses of masonry in the buttery might represent the remains of the earlier fifteenth-century range.

From the porch, a doorway would have opened on to a passage that connected with another porch on the opposite side of the building, which in turn gave access to the Fountain Court. The latter porch

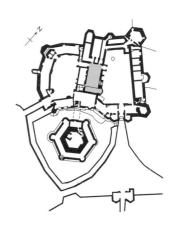

The great oriel window that lit the high table at the dais end of the hall.

Right: The interior of the great hall looking towards the high table at the dais end of the hall. Traces of the roofing arrangement survive in the gable wall.

Above: The windows in the hall contained stained glass decorated with family coats-of-arms, as shown in this manuscript illustration which depicts heraldry recorded at Raglan and Chepstow castles (College of Arms, Ms. R. 22, f. 79).

The much weathered plaque above the dais that bears the arms of the third earl of Worcester as a Knight of the Garter.

was originally the principal entrance to the hall at the time when Sir William ap Thomas's South Gate was the main approach to the castle. It was much altered when the Fountain Court buildings were erected by Sir William Herbert. The passage would have been divided from the main body of the hall by a timber screen, hence the screens-passage, and it was into this passage that the various doors from the buttery opened. Above, lay the minstrels' gallery with its own entrance from the first-floor rooms above the buttery.

The hall is the finest and most complete of the castle's surviving chambers and in its present form dates from the middle of the sixteenth century, though it does incorporate parts of an earlier hall. This is shown by the two blocked windows in the south-west wall, which were made redundant when Sir William Herbert added the chapel on the other side of the wall. Some of the lower courses of masonry in the gable wall, at the high table end of the hall, are also likely to date from the first half of the fifteenth century.

The great fireplace, with its divided flue running up each side of the window above it, the windows themselves, and delicately moulded roof corbels, are all part of the work carried out by the third earl of Worcester. This rebuilding may have been completed by 1570. It is likely that the walls of the hall had timber panelling or wainscot up to the line of the windows. The windows themselves included stained glass emblazoned with family coats-of-arms.

The plaque above the dais set into an earlier window, and now somewhat weathered, bears the arms of the third earl of Worcester as a Knight of the Garter (after 1570). In the nineteenth century the motto of the Order of the Garter, *Honi soit qui mal y pense*, was still visible surrounding the arms, as was the Somerset family motto, *Mutare vel timere sperno* (I scorn to change or fear).

The hall was described in the seventeenth century as 'having a rare geometrical roof built of Irish oak, with a large cupola on the top for light', and it remained standing for over twenty years after the siege. The slots for the wall posts of this roof are visible above the corbels, and these, together with the curving line of plaster on the gable above the dais, are an indication that its design was akin to the double hammer-beam roof of the hall of the Middle Temple in London (1562–70). The third earl of Worcester was a contributor to the cost of the Middle Temple hall, and his coat-of-arms was placed in one of the windows upon completion of the building.

At the dais end of the hall are the remains of a doorway that led to a staircase, which may have risen to the upper floors of the state apartments and long gallery, and also to a passage connecting the hall with what became the parlour. Prior to construction of this passage, there was a door in the gable wall behind the dais, but this has been blocked on the hall side and is now only visible from the parlour (p. 47). Access to these private chambers was probably limited to persons of appropriate rank and status, given the position of the doorways so close to the high table.

The surviving doorway also gave access to the cellars below the Fountain Court; it is here that the main wine cellars would have been located.

Above: The Middle Temple hall in London. The third earl of Worcester contributed to the cost of its construction and the double hammer-beam roof may resemble that at Raglan, which is known to have had 'a rare geometrical roof, built of Irish oak' during the Tudor period (By courtesy of the Honourable Society of the Middle Temple).

Left: An artist's impression of the hall as remodelled by the third earl of Worcester. To the right is the high table, at which the earl might have been present on great ceremonial occasions, but which was more usually occupied by senior household officials. Musicians doubtless performed on the gallery above the screens-passage (Illustration by Ivan Lapper, 1993; with modifications, 2003).

The Fountain Court

The Fountain Court retains its fifteenth-century arrangement of finely appointed apartments. It takes its name, however, from a fountain which was probably installed late in the sixteenth century.

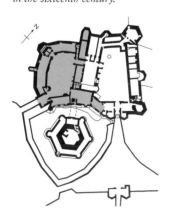

Entering the Fountain Court from the hall via the porch, the contrast with the functional nature of the Pitched Stone Court is clear. Here, you are faced with no less than four superb suites of late medieval residential accommodation, albeit ruinous, built by Sir William Herbert for his family and guests. Opposite is the grand stair, which gave access to pairs of chambers on each side at ground and first-floor level. To the left is the South Gate and a third suite of well-appointed apartments that overlooked the moat. Tucked into the corner, behind the hall, are the state apartments and nearby is a set of steps leading to the bridge to the Great Tower, where there was yet more accommodation. Each chamber was equipped for comfort with fireplaces, attractive windows with seats and access to private latrines. Moreover, the survival of an intricately decorated first-floor window near the South Gate indicates the high standard of workmanship employed on these lodging suites.

The Fountain Court itself took its later name from a 'pleasant marble fountain in the midst thereof, called the White Horse, continually running with clear water'. Fragments of the fountain, which is likely to have been of late Tudor date, still survived in the eighteenth century but only the base now remains in the centre of the court. The White Horse would have been an appropriate embellishment for the fourth earl of Worcester, who was Master of the Horse to both Elizabeth I and James I (pp. 16–17).

Above: One of the fifteenth-century corbels in the chapel — finely carved in the shape of a human head.

Left: The remains of the chapel in the Fountain Court. The one surviving wall is shared with the hall. The curving stairs are probably a Tudor addition and gave access to a private gallery or closet.

The Chapel

Adjacent to the hall is the site of the fifteenth-century chapel, which was presumably entered from the porch. Three of its walls are now reduced almost to foundation level, and the fourth is shared with the hall. Traces of the stone-vaulted roof remain at one end, springing from corbels in the form of human heads. The recess with three rows of sockets may have taken the supports for a timber pew, whilst to the left the curved recess marks the site of the Tudor staircase leading from the body of the chapel. It is probable that even in the fifteenth century there were stairs here that gave access to a closet — an upper gallery that provided private seating for the lord and his family. In the will of Sir William Herbert (1469), arrangements were made for his burial in the priory at Abergavenny, although he was actually interred at Tintern Abbey. Amongst the instructions in the will for work at Abergavenny was one that the window glass should depict 'the stories of the passion of Christ and of the nativity and the Saints of mine that be in my Clozett at Ragland'.

The chapel was floored with tiles, several examples of which have been found, the majority being contemporary with Herbert's building. Some idea of the chapel's contents is given in an inventory made after Sir Walter Herbert's death in 1507 (p. 12):

a vestyment of violet; two fruntis of aulters of crymysen velvet with flours of gold; a small frunte of cloth of gold; a lytell chales of silver; a prynted mas-boke.

In the seventeenth century the castle had a chaplain as well as a chorister, or gentleman of the chapel.

A fifteenth-century floor tile recovered from the chapel area during clearance work at Raglan. The overall design of the floor, gleaming with bright yellows and golden-browns, would no doubt have been very striking.

The Tudor long gallery occupied the second floor adjacent to the hall range and ran the full length of the Fountain Court, with massive windows overlooking the gardens and great lake to the north of the castle. Long galleries were built initially for recreation purposes but soon became an indication of status and therefore a necessary attribute for any great Elizabethan house.

The Long Gallery

Little remains of what must have been one of the finest rooms of the Tudor rebuilding: the long gallery. Initially built to allow indoor recreation, long galleries increasingly became an indication of status by virtue of their length, position and decoration. The magnificence of that at Raglan can be guessed at from the still impressive, but ruinous, great end windows that look out to the hills beyond, and by the remains of an ornate Renaissance fireplace, elaborately decorated with two human figures or caryatids. The design of these sculptures is clearly taken from Hugues Sambin's *La Diversité des Termes* (1572), a copy of which still exists inscribed by the third earl of Worcester. The gallery had a series of windows overlooking the Fountain Court, and the interior probably had timber panelling. It is known from an entry in the diary of Richard Symonds for 1645 that the gallery was lined with pictures of the family of the earls of Worcester, including the first and second earls, and it is possible that the portrait of the third earl of Worcester, now at Badminton, was

Right: Part of the ornate Renaissance fireplace in the long gallery, decorated with two human figures, or caryatids.

Far right: The design for the caryatids at Raglan, which was taken from Hugues Sambin's La Diversité des Termes *(1572) (RIBA Library Drawings Collection).*

Left: An artist's impression of the long gallery as it may have looked during the late Elizabethan period. It is shown with the walls hung with tapestries and paintings, with some areas of wood panelling (Illustration by Ivan Lapper, 1993; with modifications, 2003).

Below: The fifteenth-century porch and grand stair leading to apartments in the Fountain Court.

among them. By way of comparison, in 1643 the gallery at the marquis of Worcester's London house is known to have contained twenty-one pictures with frames and twenty-eight pictures without.

Below the western end of the gallery were other rooms, including a cellar (p. 35) and a first-floor room provided with a latrine. The main entrance to this floor and the long gallery above was via the staircase inserted between the gallery and the fifteenth-century apartments around the Fountain Court, the construction of which blocked one of the earlier windows.

The Grand Stair and Apartments

The Grand Stair

The stair is approached through a monumental ornamented outer portal, and it gives some idea of how the porch to the hall may have looked in the fifteenth century. The scroll motif here, together with other carved stonework in the

Building Materials Used at Raglan

The late sixteenth-century square headed windows at Raglan are made from Bath Stone, set in rubble walling of Old Red Sandstone, which distinguishes the Tudor work from the pale fifteenth-century sandstone ashlar.

The main stone used in the construction of the castle is sandstone, but of two different types. The fifteenth-century work is characterized by the use of pale, almost yellowish sandstone. The source of this stone is known to be at Redbrook on the Wye, 3 miles (4.4km) south-east of Monmouth. The other sandstone, used in the Tudor work, is local Old Red Sandstone and can be red, brown or purplish in colour. However, a paler stone was also used in the fireplaces. The square-headed windows of the late sixteenth century are Bath Stone. Sandstone is easy to carve and dress, and hence the high quality of the work in the fifteenth-century castle, but the Tudors simply used the Old Red Sandstone in coursed rubble walling.

The use of brick instead of stone for building in Monmouthshire does not normally begin until the second half of the seventeenth century. The finest example of that period is Tredegar House, near Newport, built about 1670. At Raglan the farmhouse next to the castle must belong to about the same time; if built earlier, it is unlikely that it would have survived the 1646 siege. A handsome house in this position is depicted in Thomas Smith's paintings undertaken in the late seventeenth century (p. 18, 56). In the castle itself, however, bricks were used in vaulting throughout the later fifteenth-century work, especially in the cellars and above window openings. They were also used in the White Gate and the moat walk in the seventeenth century, and of course the Red Gate was so named from the colour of its brickwork. Though late by English standards, the use of brick by Sir William Herbert in the 1460s must rank as amongst the earliest in Wales.

Although brick can be found throughout the castle from the later fifteenth-century onwards, it does not appear in prominent locations, such as the moat walk niches (above), until the seventeenth century.

Fountain Court, suggest that craftsmen working at Raglan in the later fifteenth century may have been masons from the West Country, possibly Somerset, where other examples may be seen.

Doors on each side of the foot of the stairs led to ground-floor chambers, with a similar arrangement at the top of the staircase. Beneath the stairs are two storage rooms accessed from the ground-floor chambers. The latrines housed in the tower projecting from the back of the grand stair were reached through doors from the ground- and first-floor rooms, but the base of their chutes was later blocked by the sixteenth-century terracing built against the curtain wall.

At the top of the main steps (not currently accessible) there is a doorway. Inside there is a newel staircase, which leads up to a small room — with two windows and a fireplace — and originally carried on up to the battlements. A small turret may have covered the door onto the wall-walk.

The Apartments: North-West and South-West Ranges

The two wings on either side of the grand stair each contained at least four rooms, with two chambers on each floor. Those to the north-west (right) may have operated as two-room lodging suites on each level, with an inner and outer chamber, the room nearest the stair perhaps occupied by servants with the adjacent and more private chamber used by their master. The individual rooms in these ranges had a fireplace, two of which (on the upper floor) are well preserved. The chambers also had single light windows to the outside, each with seats in the embrasures. The courtyard frontage was more elaborate as there was a projecting square bay window of two lights as well as multiple-light windows. The rooms on both floors would have been divided from one another by timber partitions, the evidence for which has long since disappeared.

Although apparently equipped with similar window and fireplace arrangements, the lodging suites to the south-west (left) of the grand stair are more complex. There is an additional projecting latrine tower and, near the South Gate, the remains of a stair turret allowed separate access and greater privacy for this end of the range.

An artist's impression of the Fountain Court as it may have appeared soon after its completion in the 1460s. To the left is the South Gate and to the right, the porch and grand stair afford access to the adjacent apartments. It seems unlikely that the fountain that gave its name to the court was erected at this time (Illustration by Ivan Lapper, 1993; with modifications, 2003).

There was also an open passage across the back of the South Gate leading to the first floor of the south-east range. A small first-floor window survives in almost perfect condition by the South Gate, lacking only its glass.

The Apartments: South-East Range

Little remains of this residential range, alongside the South Gate, overlooking the moat and Great Tower. Raised over one of the vaulted cellars, the range was of two storeys. There was probably only one chamber on the ground floor, but perhaps two above. Bow windows originally projected both towards the Fountain Court and the moat. In the southern corner is the latrine turret, placed rather awkwardly against the South Gate and partially obscuring one of the windows lighting its stair.

Although both structures date to the fifteenth century, Sir William Herbert added the latrine turret to the earlier gate. At the opposite end of the range another stair led to the top floor, and possibly also to the bridge across the moat to the keep.

Left: One of the windows in the Fountain Court apartments. The seats in the window embrasure would have overlooked the splendid gardens below the castle.

Below: This superb first-floor window in the south-west range of apartments demonstrates the high quality of the accommodation in the Fountain Court.

The South Gate (right), built by Sir William ap Thomas between 1432 and 1445, is one of the earliest surviving parts of the castle and may have served as the main entrance to Raglan until the great gatehouse was built by his son, Sir William Herbert. Defended by a portcullis and two sets of double doors, the entrance passage was covered with elaborate fan vaulting, part of which survives in place (above).

The fan-vaulted cloisters at Gloucester Cathedral, built between 1351 and 1412, may have provided the inspiration for the vaulted gate-passage in Sir William ap Thomas's South Gate.

The South Gate

This gate was built by Sir William ap Thomas in the first half of the fifteenth century, and is referred to as the 'green gate' in 1674, leading as it did to the bowling green. The construction of the great gatehouse a few years later by Sir William Herbert, however, relegated the southern entrance to the role of a more private access to the principal apartments. Indeed, it may have been blocked at this time and reopened only when the gardens were created in the sixteenth century.

The gate had double doors at each end of the short passage, and was originally defended by a portcullis and a drawbridge over the ditch outside, which was replaced by the present fixed bridge in the sixteenth century.

There is enough evidence of the vault over the passage to show that it was an example of fan vaulting, Sir William ap Thomas's most elaborate piece of work, perhaps similar to the earlier vaulting in the cloisters at Gloucester Cathedral, built between 1351 and 1412. In one corner of the ground floor there is a stair to the upper floors and to the south-east range, whilst the corner with the fireplace may have been screened off from the passage itself to form a small chamber for the porter in the first half of the fifteenth century.

The State Apartments

The Parlour and Dining Room

Between the hall and the moat, and adjoining
the gatehouse range, were the private rooms
of the successive lords of Raglan, the state
apartments. The rooms immediately behind the
hall are named in a seventeenth-century account
as the parlour on the ground floor with the
dining room above. The parlour was noted in
the seventeenth century for its:
inlaid wainscott and curious carved figures, as also
for the rare and artificial stone work of the flat arch
in a large and fair compass window on the south side,
beaten down by the enemies' great guns, and two
neat windows at each end.
Equally, in the fifteenth century, these two chambers
may have been audience or reception areas, where
Sir William Herbert could meet and dine with
guests in greater privacy than the hall allowed.

Little remains of all this splendour, although the
carved chimney-piece and panelling brought from
Troy House to Badminton House in 1895 may have
come from this room, as well as the Cefntilla frieze
(p. 22). All that can be seen of the 'fair compass
window' is the foundation of the projecting oriel
overlooking the moat, and it would seem from the
seventeenth-century description that it was finer
than the windows in the state bedrooms which,
as we shall see, still retain much of their magnificently
carved stonework.

Of the 'two neat windows at each end', one
looked out on the Fountain Court, the other on
the Pitched Stone Court. A photograph of the
parlour and dining room windows overlooking
the Pitched Stone Court, taken at the beginning
of the last century, shows the dining room window
still in existence.

The parlour may have been the withdrawing
room of the seventeenth-century accounts. It was
here that the marquis of Worcester would have
sat with his guests after dinner. During the siege,
the marquis was sitting in this room when a
musket bullet hit the window, the spent shot then
proceeding to strike him on the head, but without
causing serious injury. The blocked doorway, which
originally led from the parlour into the hall (p. 39),
can be seen in the gable wall on this side.

An illustration from a late
fifteenth-century Flemish
manuscript depicting high status
dining arrangements in a castle.
Just one diner is seated at the
table, attended by a range of
serving staff. Similar scenes
perhaps took place in the dining
room at Raglan (Bodleian
Library, University of Oxford,
Ms. Laud Misc. 751, f. 179r).

Although much ruined and
difficult to reconstruct, the parlour
and dining room occupied the
grassed area between the hall and
moat. The two large round-headed
openings are all that remain of the
windows, which overlooked the
Pitched Stone Court. The upper
window, belonging to the dining
room, survived until the beginning
of the twentieth century and
can be seen in the top left of
this photograph (below) with its
stone tracery intact.

Although the parlour and dining room in the state apartments were destroyed after the 1646 siege, the surviving carved stonework that decorated the remaining chambers suggests that this suite was of the highest quality. Both the surviving rooms, adjacent to the gatehouse range, are likely to have served as bedchambers.

The Bedrooms

The wall dividing the parlour and the dining room from the state bedrooms has undergone considerable alteration, as has the ground-floor room entered by the door off the parlour. Although there is a fifteenth-century doorway on the first floor, little sense can be made of these alterations. They do, however, appear to be nineteenth-century work and may have been the result of the structural weakness in this area of the castle referred to earlier (p. 30). The first floor was certainly the lord's bedchamber. The beauty of the handiwork of the medieval craftsmen who carved the masonry can be fully appreciated, especially in the internal details of the windows; it may even have been this room that the marquis of Worcester 'most esteemed of all in the castle'. Although we cannot be certain how the room was furnished, it is likely to be similar to that described in a 1643 account of the marquis's London house which included tapestry hangings and *1 stope bed stede Curtaines & Vallance & tester & Counter paine of leade color Cloath laced 1 w'th buttons & loopes & silck fringe.*

One other feature of the first-floor chamber is the fireplace, which is placed in an unusual position against the top of the larger window. It is an addition of the sixteenth century, when the attic was built along this side of the castle. The floor must, therefore, have partially obscured the uppermost part of the window, hiding the decoration from the inside. Presumably this was felt to be a small price to pay for the advantage of having another floor.

The ground floor, possibly another bedroom, has lost the elaborate decoration of its windows, but still has one moulded jamb of a much altered fifteenth-century fireplace in the opposite wall. Running along the present floor level is the top of the brick vault of the cellar below.

The Great Tower

The Great Tower can be regarded as a defensive stronghold in its own right, certainly as originally built. Self-contained, with its own kitchen and water supply, surrounded by a moat, initially it was only accessible from the main part of the castle by passing over a double drawbridge arrangement. Yet its role was much more than this. It was, like any other great tower, a mark of status, to be seen from miles around, particularly for a family that had risen from the ranks of local Welsh gentry. It was also a well-appointed private residence, with latrines and fireplaces at all levels, designed for comfort and gracious living.

The Bridge to the Great Tower

A short flight of steps leads up to a modern bridge constructed in 1957 on the line of its late medieval predecessor. At the top of the steps is a doorway, with the remains of a window above it, which itself has traces of another opening over it, best seen from the bridge. The doorway led to the 'sumptuous arched bridge,' constructed in the fifteenth century, though it may have been remodelled by the Somersets, for the 1674 description of the castle mentions that the bridge cost £900 or £1,000.

Before entering the keep, two features should be noticed. First, the intricate carved masonry above the windows of the state apartments emphasizes the lavish display initiated by Herbert on the castle. The windows are framed between shafts running up their full length, ending in carved pinnacles, and above are heraldic motifs of shields and badges. The latter are in the form of bascule drawbridges, the type of bridge originally used by Sir William ap Thomas as the means of entry into the keep (see below). The bascule was a badge of the Herberts and was used in a seventeenth-century copy of a seal to a Raglan deed dated 1451. The design is also to be seen above the entrance to one of the fifteenth-century porches of St Mary's Church, Usk, and in the Beaufort Chapel in St George's Chapel, Windsor Castle.

Alternating with the badges are shields, which may once have been painted with family coats-of-arms. Richard Symonds mentions in his diary for 1645 that a coat-of-arms, which included the three lions rampant of the Herberts, was 'carved, old, on the wall of the outside'.

The second feature to note is the change in the methods of entry into the Great Tower itself, both dating to the fifteenth century (see reconstruction drawings overleaf). When the Great Tower was first built, by Sir William ap Thomas, a timber bridge led from the court to two rectangular stone piers on the other side of the moat. The gap between the timber bridge and the keep was spanned by a pair of drawbridges of a type known as a bascule. This type was particularly common in Europe, and can be seen at Herstmonceux in Sussex and Bothwell in Scotland, but the paired arrangement at Raglan is unique in Britain.

The three vertical grooves allowed the supporting arms of the bridges to fit flush against the wall when the bridges were raised. These drawbridges meant that in times of trouble, Sir William ap Thomas could isolate himself completely from the rest of the castle, and in some comfort as the keep had its own kitchen and water supply. The arrangement was not, however, to last for long. Sir William Herbert removed his father's drawbridges and the timber bridge across the moat, and built the sumptuous stone bridge referred to above. The stone bridge was of a single span and led to a three-storey building added to the front of the keep, blocking the earlier drawbridge arrangements. Only the foundations of this forebuilding survive, but the abutment for the stone bridge incorporates the two piers of the earlier timber structure.

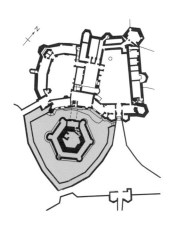

A detail of the carved stonework above the windows of the state apartments. The badge (left) depicts a bascule bridge and the shield (right), though now colourless, may have been painted with the family coat-of-arms.

Left: The approach to the bridge that crossed the moat to the Great Tower.

The Great Tower

A reconstruction of the Great Tower, with the bascule bridge arrangements, as first built by Sir William ap Thomas. The top of the tower is shown restored with crenellations. It may, however, have carried elaborate machicolations in the contemporary French style, as shown in the opposite drawing (Illustration by Chris Jones-Jenkins, 1993).

Turning to the details of the Great Tower, we must at once appreciate that it presents a sadly reduced picture of its former glory. In the seventeenth century, one observer noted that 'on the left side stood the Tower of Gwent, which for height, strength and neatness, surpassed most, if not every other tower of England or Wales'. This was no exaggeration. The same commentator also tells us that the keep had a fifth floor, and there are likely to have been machicolated battlements above this.

But after the siege of 1646, during which the tower itself 'repulsed bullets of 18 and 20lb in weight,

hardly receiving the least impression by sixty shot a day', the top floor was systematically demolished. Because of the time that was taken in 'tedious battering the top thereof with pickaxes', the tower was undermined, resulting in the collapse of its walls. The parliamentarian artillery had already destroyed the vulnerable battlements. No wonder its grandeur is somewhat diminished today.

At bridge level, there are two doors that were the original entrances into the keep, the smaller of which was later converted into a fireplace, with the original drawbridge socket used for the chimney flue. The roof-line of the now-destroyed forebuilding built by Sir William Herbert is marked by a horizontal joint for the lead running across the face of the tower. Rising above the level of this roof-line, an original window between two sockets for the main drawbridge was enlarged to allow more light into the tower, as part of it would have been obscured by the forebuilding. Lower down and to the left is another door, opening onto the staircase. The purpose of this was to connect the tower with the upper floor of the forebuilding.

After passing across the site of the forebuilding, and in through the main door, you stand in a small vestibule or lobby. It was from here that the original bascule bridges would have been worked. The two doors opposite led into the great chamber.

The existing upper floor of the Great Tower provides a magnificent view of the whole of the castle, and the interior of the tower itself. Views can also be had of the Civil War earthworks around the castle. On the high ground, beyond the farm, you can still see the slight traces of the parliamentarian gun battery, enclosing a modern water tank. In the corner of the field near the entrance to the car park, there is a pointed artillery bastion, with traces of the rampart, both part of the defences added by the marquis of Worcester during the Civil War (pp. 19–20).

As for the internal arrangements of the tower, these can best be appreciated from the basement kitchen. Here, the cobbling is modern. The kitchen would have been very dark, the only natural light coming from the gunloops and the cross-slits. The grooves running back from the oillets or holes of the horizontal arms of the slits enabled greater light to penetrate. No doubt candles or torches were used for additional lighting.

The room contains a large fireplace where the wall of the keep was brought down, and there is a well in one of the gun embrasures. The well mechanism must have made the embrasure useless as a gun position. A small door leads into the well-preserved medieval latrine, there being one such latrine on each floor. The corbels in the wall supported vertical timbers, which in turn supported the floor above, and this arrangement is to be seen on the other floors.

The small enclosed chamber in the kitchen was added at a later date and may have housed the castle treasury, including the silver and gilt plate. An inventory of the plate in the Great Tower made in 1639 lists over 290 items of silver plate and over seventy more of gilt. These included great and little dishes, candlesticks, salts, tankards, a container for oranges and lemons, a chamber pot, two hot-water bottles and an ink pot.

The room above the kitchen was the great chamber. It was furnished with a plain fireplace, and its windows are only single lights. In one wall there is simply a cross-slit. Notice that the size of the windows increases the higher one goes up inside the tower, reflecting the status of the rooms, the best window being reserved for the lord's private accommodation, which would have been located on the upper floors.

The next floor has an ornamental fireplace, and there are large two-light windows with seats in the

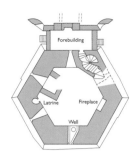

Basement — kitchen

First floor — great chamber

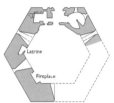

Second floor

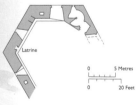

0   5 Metres

0   20 Feet

Third floor

A reconstruction of the Great Tower and bridge as they might have appeared at the time of Sir William Herbert. The machicolated battlements are based on those seen elsewhere at the castle, but could have taken the simpler form shown opposite (Illustration by Chris Jones-Jenkins, 1993; with modifications, 2003).

embrasures. The brick niches in one of these embrasures are an addition of the early seventeenth century, at the same time as the niches were added to the walk on the other side of the moat. Presumably the upper rooms were still regarded in the seventeenth century as favourite accommodation by the Somersets. The bedroom lay on the floor above, where there are both single and double light windows, and the destroyed top storey may also have been a bedchamber.

The Apron Wall

Returning to the staircase, a few steps up from the kitchen, there is a door added by Sir William Herbert. This leads into the site of the forebuilding, and so out to the apron wall surrounding the keep. It might be assumed that the wall was built at the same time as the tower, but the fact that in its original battlemented state it would have obscured the gunloops in the walls of the kitchen implies that the apron was part of the later fifteenth-century additions. The wall had six corner turrets, one of which has a latrine, and another a postern door to the moat. The turrets have cross-slits, one with a drain below it, but there is no evidence for gunloops.

Opposite: The Great Tower — the Yellow Tower of Gwent — remains one of the most striking features of Raglan and continues to inspire debate about its origin and function. The internal arrangements, floor by floor, are clearly visible through the breach created by parliamentarian troops in the seventeenth century.

Left: One of the six turrets in the apron wall that surrounds the Great Tower. The postern gate would have allowed access to the moat, which was perhaps stocked with fish.

Great Towers in the Later Middle Ages

From the eleventh century, great towers, or keeps, dominated castle enclosures. Intended as military strongholds, they also served as self-contained houses, but above all they were symbols of power and lordship. By the thirteenth century, however, the military and domestic limitations of the keep led to the development of the curtain wall castle in which accommodation could be arranged in lodgings inside the enclosure or in towers included in the circuit of the curtain walls. Like the earlier keeps, towers conferred status and authority and it may have been this expression of lordship that made the great tower popular again from the late fourteenth century, but now they were more likely to be equipped for comfort than for defence.

Forms and circumstances varied: for example, the great brick tower at Tattershall in Lincolnshire, dating to around 1432–48, was probably built as an elaborate extension of the accommodation within an earlier castle, a mark of Ralph, Lord Cromwell's status as Treasurer of England. On the other hand, the Great Tower at Raglan and, to some extent, that built by William, Lord Hastings from around 1474 at Ashby de la Zouch, Leicestershire, seem to have been more military in purpose. Nevertheless, in spite of the troubled times of the Wars of the Roses, there is no reason to suppose that the sole function of these great towers was military, any more than those built at Warwick in the fourteenth century or the magnificent late fourteenth-century tower at Warkworth in Northumberland.

Great towers continued to be built into the sixteenth century, but as the Tudor machinery of government gradually imposed stability and reduced the power of great magnates, so the need for towers of imposing military character declined. Domestic comfort as well as status were to be served better by the development of the country house.

The great brick tower at Tattershall Castle, Lincolnshire. Although similar in date to Raglan's Great Tower, Tattershall seems to be less military in character and was probably built to provide additional accommodation (National Trust Photographic Library: Andrew Butler).

The Garden Outworks and Buildings

One of fifteen brick niches built into the moat walk by the fourth earl of Worcester. The niches originally housed highly fashionable statues of Roman emperors and were decorated with coloured plasterwork and shells, traces of which are still visible.

The steep grassy banks at the back of the castle hint at the elaborate garden terraces created by the earls of Worcester. Remarkably, earthwork evidence of the magnificent water gardens also survives in the valley floor beyond.

The landscape around the immediate environs of the castle represents what has been recognized as one of the most important surviving Renaissance gardens in Britain, laid out at the time of the third, fourth and fifth earls of Worcester (1550–1646). In the Elizabethan and early Stuart periods, extensive gardens incorporating Renaissance features such as fountains and sculpture became essential attributes of any great courtier's home. Raglan, with its water features, parterres, knot gardens and terracing, was at the very forefront of these developments. The abandonment of the castle after the Civil War has meant that the gardens were left largely untouched and overgrown, but their structure — as shown in Laurence Smythe's plan of 1652 (p. 14) — can be traced in earthworks on the ground.

An appreciation of these features can best be made by leaving the castle through the South Gate.

The Moat Walk

The moat walk around the Great Tower, created by the fourth earl of Worcester, can be reached from under the bridge to the South Gate. Fifteen brick-built niches enhance the walk. These were originally decorated with shells and coloured plasterwork, traces of which survive, and contained figures of Roman emperors. Passing under the now-blocked bridge would have provided access from the moat walk to the parkland beyond the White Gate shown in Thomas Smith's late seventeenth-century painting (p. 56).

The Bowling Green

The raised terrace adjoining the South Gate bridge, overlooking the moat walk, was used later in the castle's history as a bowling green. King Charles I played bowls here when he stayed with the marquis in 1645, and was one of the last people to enjoy the castle gardens in their heyday. The green was connected to the terrace in front of the gatehouse across the now-blocked single-arched bridge.

The Terraces

In the corner of the terrace, opposite the South Gate, a flight of steps leads down to the site of what was perhaps the 'garden plot' (now occupied by maintenance huts), in the north-western corner of which are the foundations of a brick summerhouse. This is the area that the fourth earl of Worcester may have remodelled on the lines of his garden at Worcester Lodge at Nonsuch (p. 17). There are further terraces to the west, the lowest of which was accessed by a flight of steps that still survives. Beyond are the areas described on Smythe's map as the hopyard and warren.

The most impressive terraces survive at the back of the castle. Here, there are the remains of four terraces, which were originally revetted with stone walls and stone balustrades, similar to those that can still be seen at Haddon Hall, Derbyshire. Flights of steps would have linked the various levels, which would have been laid out with gravel paths and

flowerbeds arranged in the sixteenth century as formal patterns or 'knots', but later simplified. No doubt statuary would also have been added as it became fashionable in the early seventeenth century.

Walking along the top terrace, note the two projecting latrine towers of the Fountain Court, the chutes of which were blocked as a result of the construction of the terraces. The north-western frontage is dominated by the new work of the third earl of Worcester, distinguished by the red rubble masonry (though probably rendered originally), including the long gallery and adjacent stair turret. At ground level, note the bases of two Tudor latrines. Beyond the stair turret the difference between the masonry that marks the junction of Sir William Herbert's work (to the left) and that of the earls of Worcester (to the right) is especially clear (p. 12, 34).

The Water Gardens

Below the long terraces was a large lake — the 'great poole' — formed by damming the Wilcae brook. The bed of this lake is still visible, filling the valley floor, although a line of trees divides its original area into two. Not only would this have supplied fish for the household but it could also be used for entertainments. In the early seventeenth century a formal water garden — or water parterre — was created at the head of the lake. This was a very advanced feature for its time and few were made in Britain. It was a rectangular area laid out in diamond-shaped islands with water channels between them and can be seen in the meadow, below the Kitchen Tower, as mounds and boggy channels. Close to it lie the overgrown remains of another summerhouse.

An artist's impression of how the gardens at Raglan and the surrounding landscaped parkland may have looked in the early years of the seventeenth century. The form of the summerhouse on the upper terrace is based on its ground plan and on the distant summerhouse that appears in Thomas Smith's painting of about 1684 (p. 18). The form of the second summerhouse is more conjectural (Illustration by Ivan Lapper, 2003).

A late seventeenth-century painting of Raglan, by Thomas Smith, showing the Red Gate and formal drive to the castle, almost nothing of which now survives (His grace, the duke of Beaufort).

The White Gate

This dates from the early seventeenth century and was not built as a defensive structure. Today, only the basement and part of the ground-floor walling survive. The gate was constructed largely of brick and Old Red Sandstone, with paler sandstone used for the finer details, including the scallop-headed niches and windows. The approach to this gate was through an outer enclosure — now occupied by much of the car park. This in turn was entered through the Red Gate, which overlooked landscaped parkland and a formal approach to the castle consisting of a straight drive that crossed a 'double' pond over a central bridge. A second, less formal road approached from the west. A record of these arrangements appears in Thomas Smith's late seventeenth-century painting (left).

The White Gate was one of the last additions to Raglan, probably at the beginning of the seventeenth century, and is now the main entrance to the castle.

Further Reading

Acknowledgements
The author and Cadw would like to thank Rees Davies, Ralph Griffiths, Stephen Priestley and Elisabeth Whittle for their help in the preparation of this edition of the guidebook. The information on the Cefntilla frieze is taken from John Morgan-Guy's description and analysis, kindly provided by Thomas Lloyd.

R. A. Brown, *English Castles*, 3rd ed. (London 1976).

A. Clark, *Raglan Castle and the Civil War in Monmouthshire* (Chepstow 1953).

B. Coplestone-Crow, 'Strongbow's Grant of Raglan to Walter Bluet', *Gwent Local History* **89** (2000), 3–27.

H. Durant, *Raglan Castle* (Risca 1980).

A. Emery, 'The Development of Raglan Castle and Keeps in Late Medieval England', *Archaeological Journal* **132** (1975), 151–86.

A. Emery, *Greater Medieval Houses of England and Wales 1300–1500. 2. East Anglia, Central England, and Wales* (Cambridge 2000).

H. T. Evans, *Wales and the Wars of the Roses* (Stroud 1995; first published 1915).

M. Girouard, *Life in the English Country House: A Social and Architectural History* (New Haven 1978).

R. Haslam, 'Raglan and After: The Seventeenth-Century Welsh Houses of the Beauforts', *Country Life* **183:45** (1989), 96–101.

D. Howarth, *Lord Arundel and his Circle* (New Haven 1985).

M. Johnson, *Behind the Castle Gate: From Medieval to Renaissance* (London 2002).

J. R. Kenyon, 'The Civil War Earthworks around Raglan Castle, Gwent: An Aerial View', *Archaeologia Cambrensis* **131**, (1982), 139–42.

J. R. Kenyon, 'The Gunloops at Raglan Castle, Gwent', in J. R. Kenyon and R. Avent, editors, *Castles in Wales and the Marches* (Cardiff 1987), 161–72.

J. M. Lewis, 'The Chapel at Raglan Castle and its Paving Tiles', in J. R. Kenyon and R. Avent, editors, *Castles in Wales and the Marches* (Cardiff 1987), 143–60.

R. Strong, *The Cult of Elizabeth: Elizabethan Portraiture and Pageantry* (London 1977).

R. Strong, *The Renaissance Garden in England* (London 1979).

R. Strong, *The Artist & the Garden* (New Haven 2000).

A. J. Taylor, *Raglan Castle, Gwent*, 14th impression (HMSO, Cardiff 1979).

D. H. Thomas, *The Herberts of Raglan and the Battle of Edgecote 1469* (Enfield 1994).

M. W. Thompson, *The Decline of the Castle* (Cambridge 1987).

E. Whittle, 'The Renaissance Gardens of Raglan Castle', *Garden History* **17** (1989), 83–94.

E. Whittle, *The Historic Gardens of Wales* (London 1992).

G. Williams, *Recovery, Reorientation and Reformation: Wales c. 1415–1642* (Oxford 1987); reprinted in paperback as *Renewal and Reformation: Wales c. 1415–1642* (Oxford 1993).

C. M. Woolgar, *The Great Household in Late Medieval England* (New Haven 1999).